Dark Starlight Publications Presents

Florida's Most Beautiful Sunsets

By

Patti Chiappa

Dark Starlight Publications

2605 Legend Ct

Leesburg, FL 34748

Ordering Information:

Quantity sales. Special discounts are available on quantity purchases by corporations, associations, and others. For details, contact the publisher at the address above.

Orders by U.S. trade bookstores and wholesalers. Contact: Soulbabylondon@gmail.com

Printed in the United States of America 2016

All Pictures Taken By Patti Chiappa.

Dedicated to all those who have sunshine in their souls. For Diane

Sunsets-It's as if the colors and intensity of the light is just enough to calm you. The sun is like a great big romantic, inspirational fire in the sky. It would be as if a powerful symphony was quieting down, becoming more emotional and beautiful as it dies down.

Its rays seem friendly. They remind me of an old friend, waving good bye to you, you know they are leaving but you are filled with the confidence that you will see them again.

The Sunset is like a great joy and relaxation after a long day and its colors will give you the warmth to comfort you to exhale in a calmly mood to recover energies for the next day; It is the Anticipation for the Dawn that with the Sunlight will lift you up to start a new day of life!

It's an awesome scene before us. It feels like a soothing, a relaxation after a hot, loud, noisy and tiresome day. This soothing and relaxing music's are further leading towards a silence, a silence of peace, warmth and love. The scene is lovely, eternal moment from this transition

Sunsets- it's like the comforting warmth of a sweet embrace, stilling your heart, and causing your breath to hold for the slightest of moments as the wonderment of the beauty of it collects in a bag of mixed emotions, leaving you to feel a true sense of joy in the end.

This book captures some of the most amazing sunsets photographed around the state of Florida by Patti Chiappa.

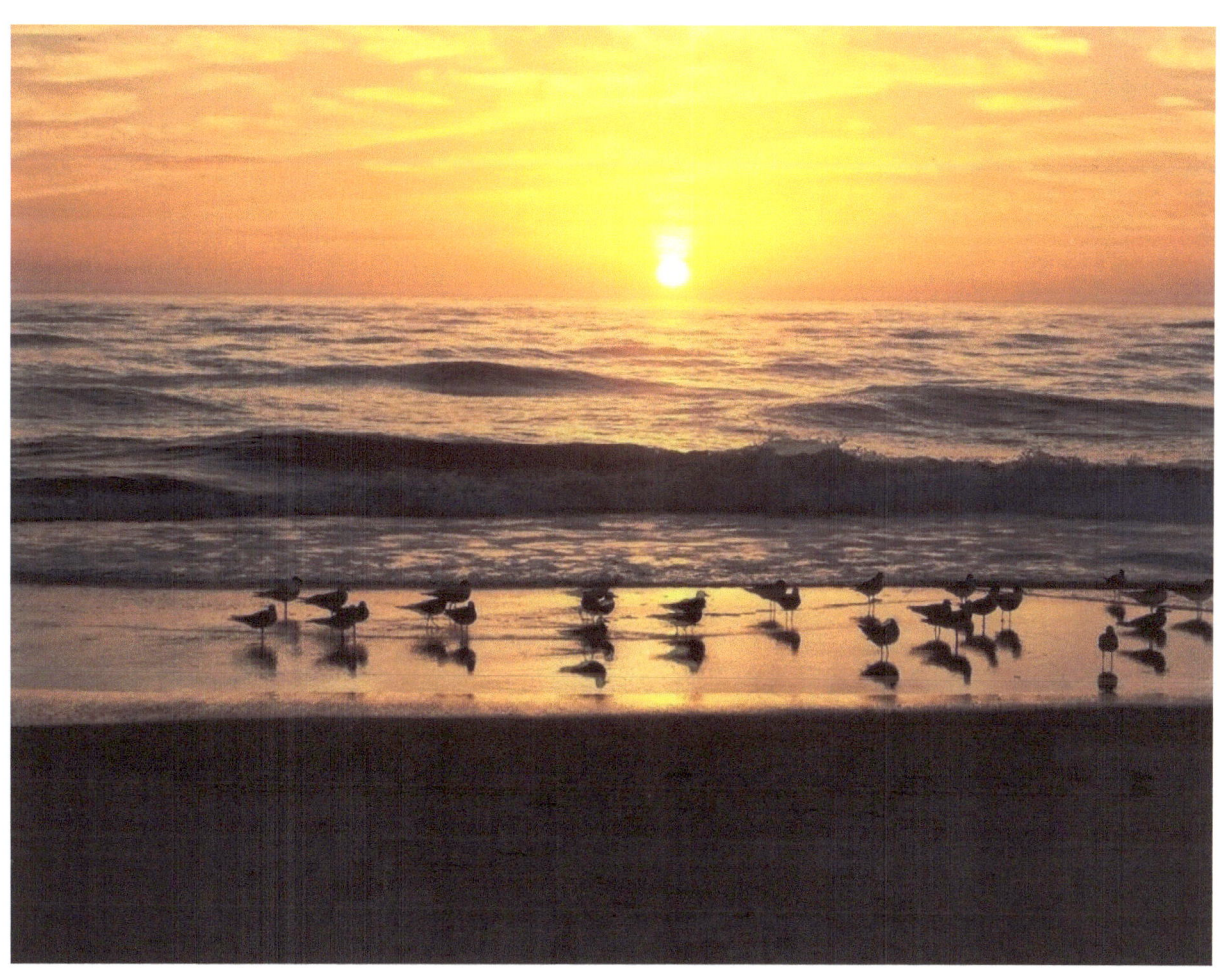

Port Richey- Florida

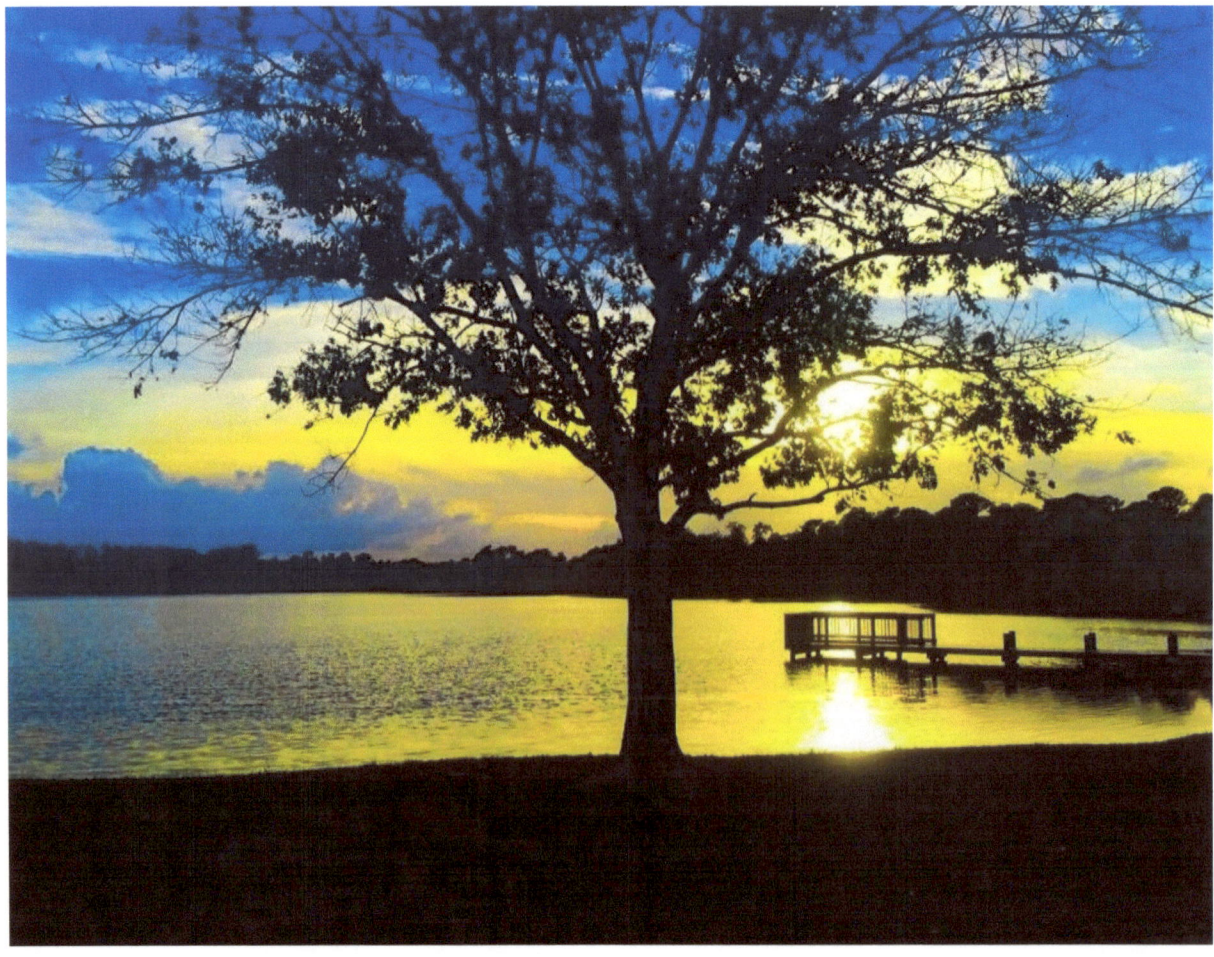

Clearwater Beach Florida

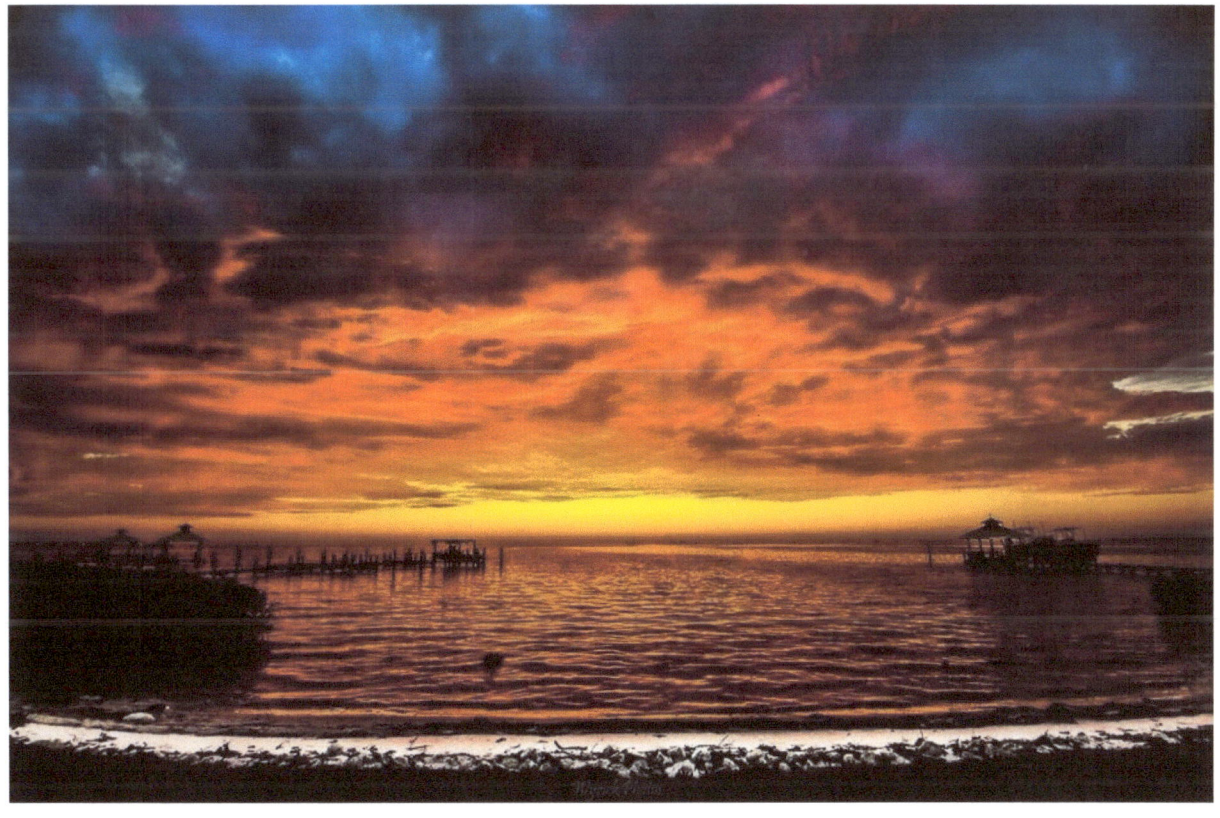

Melbourne Florida

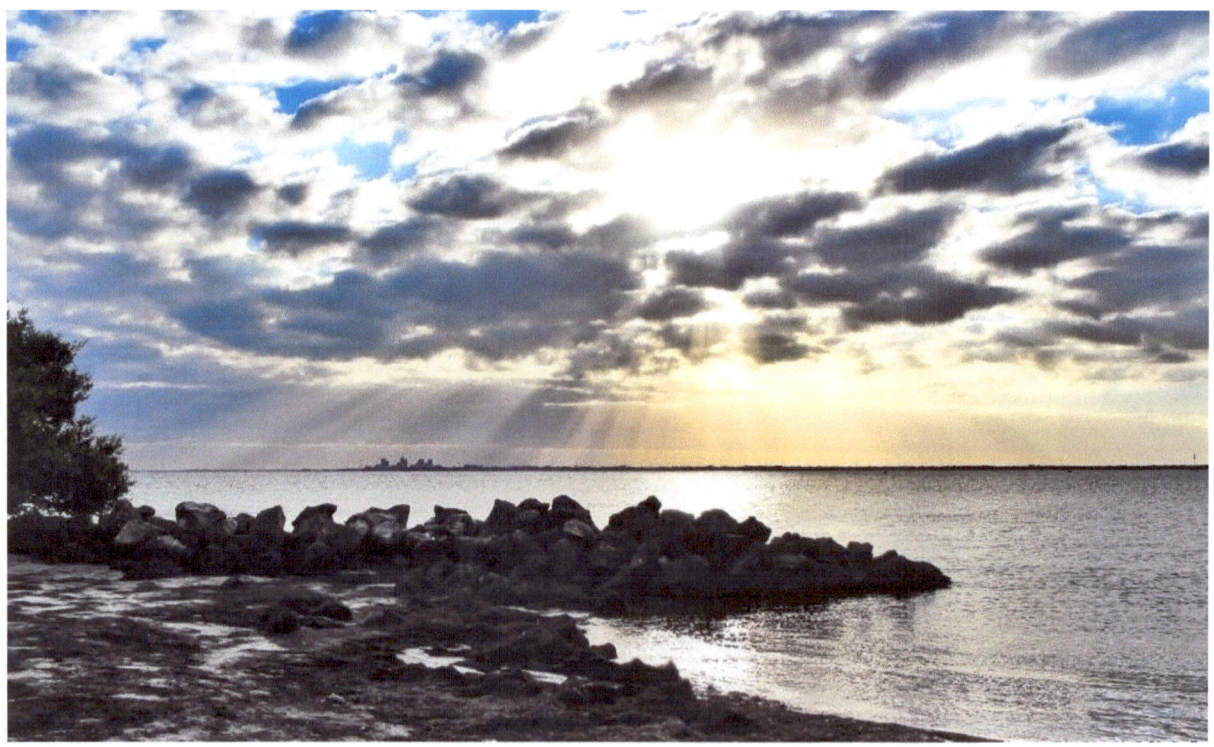

Tampa Florida

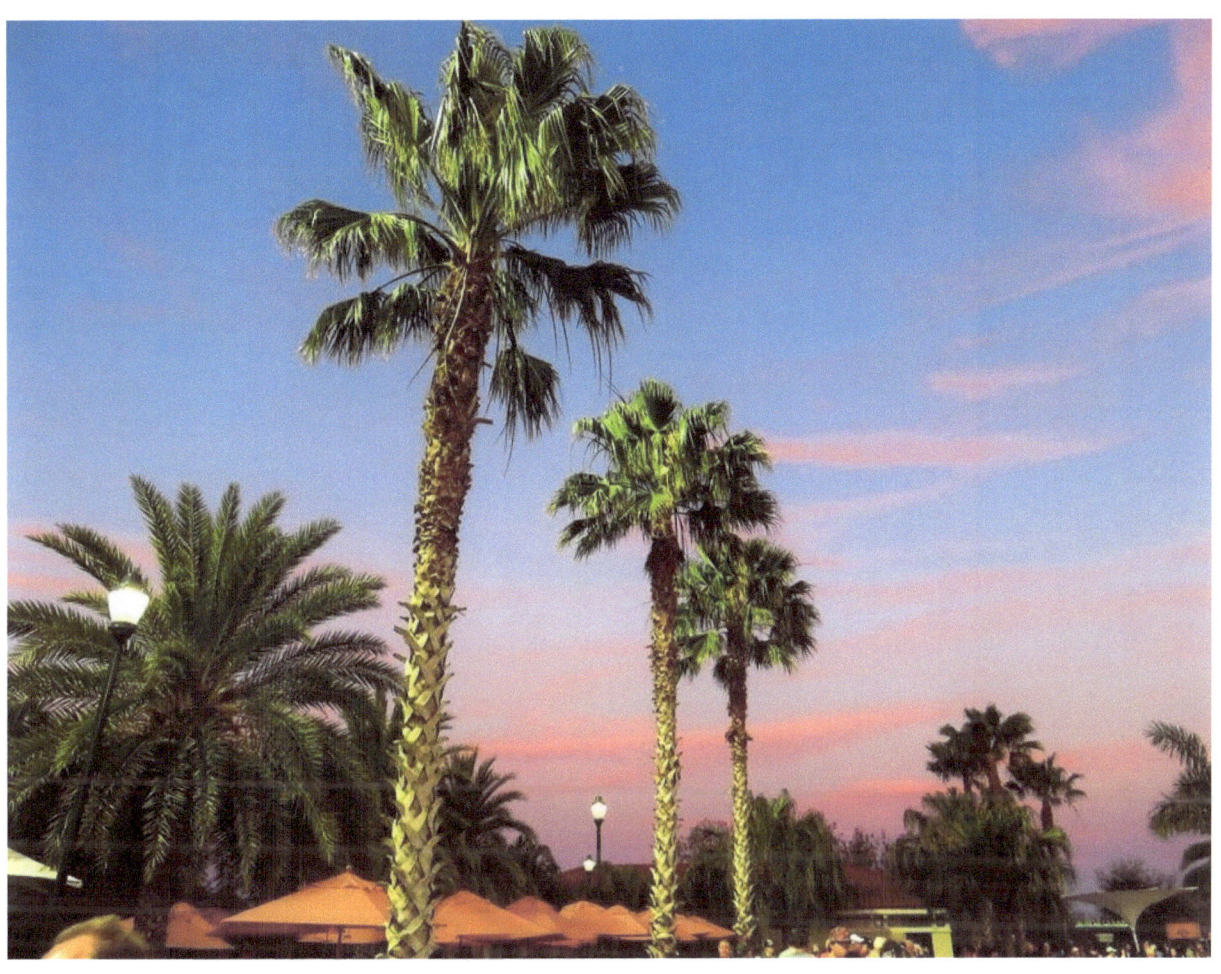

Daytona Beach FL

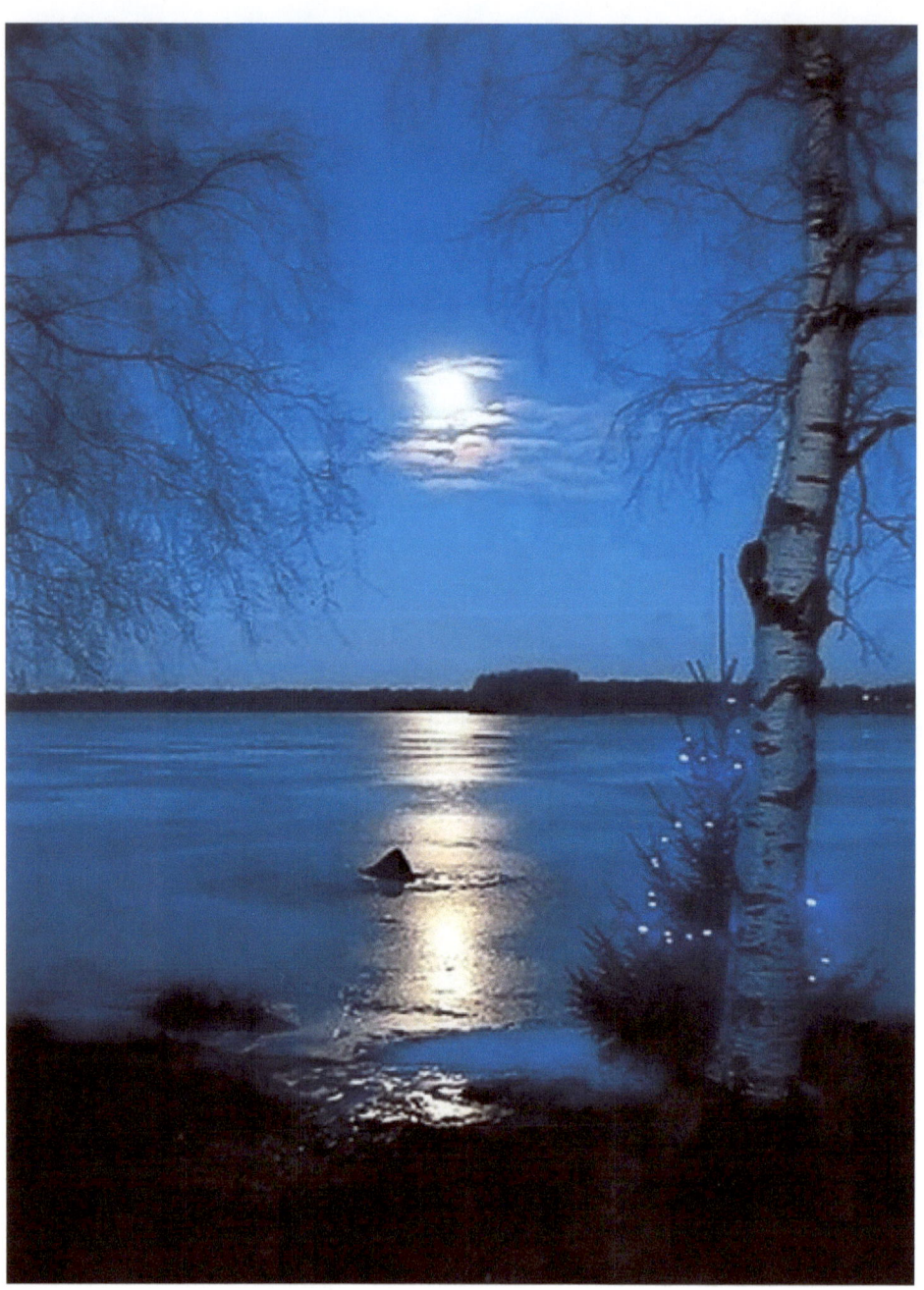

Lake Wales Florida

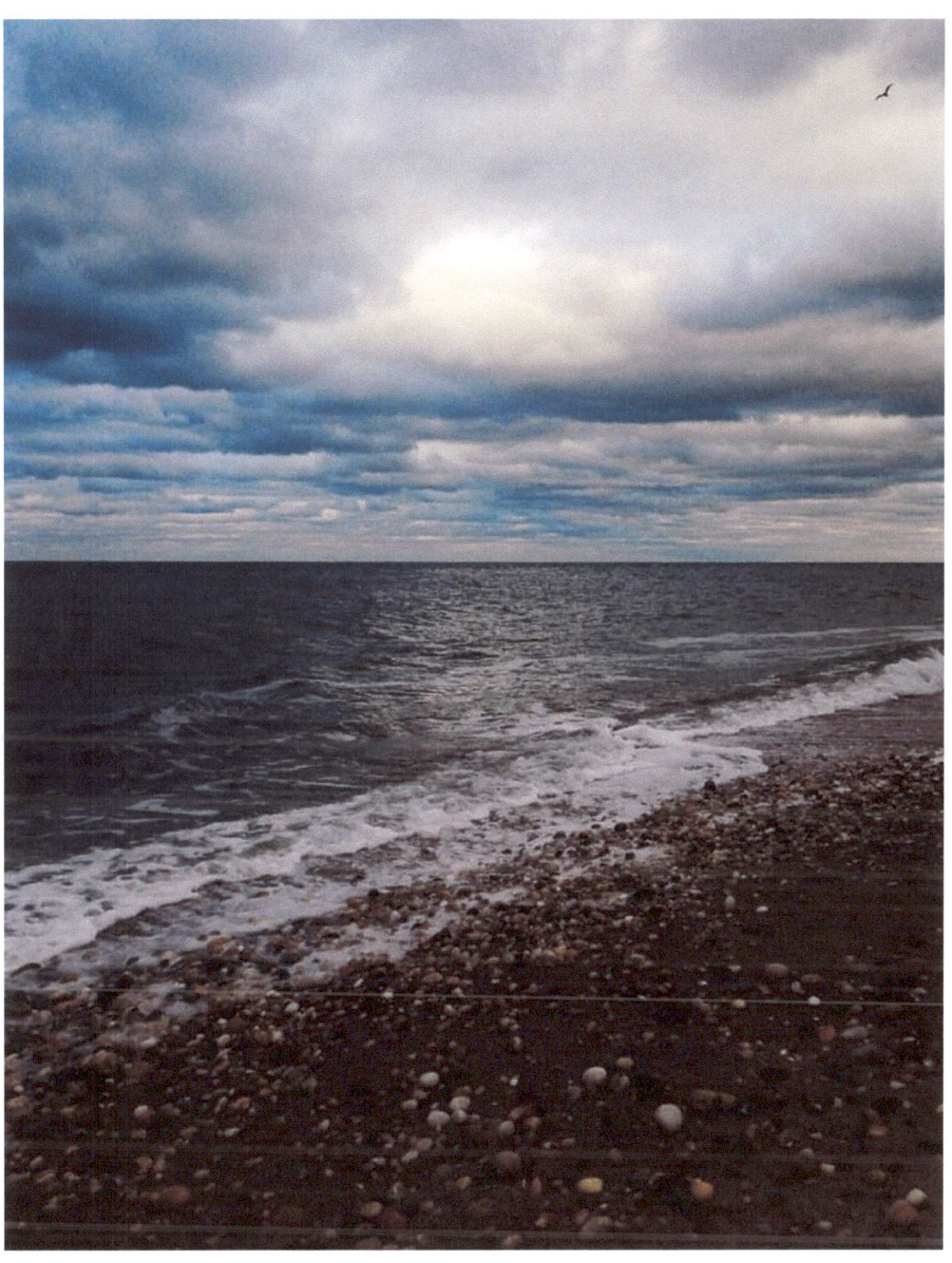

Clearwater Beach Florida

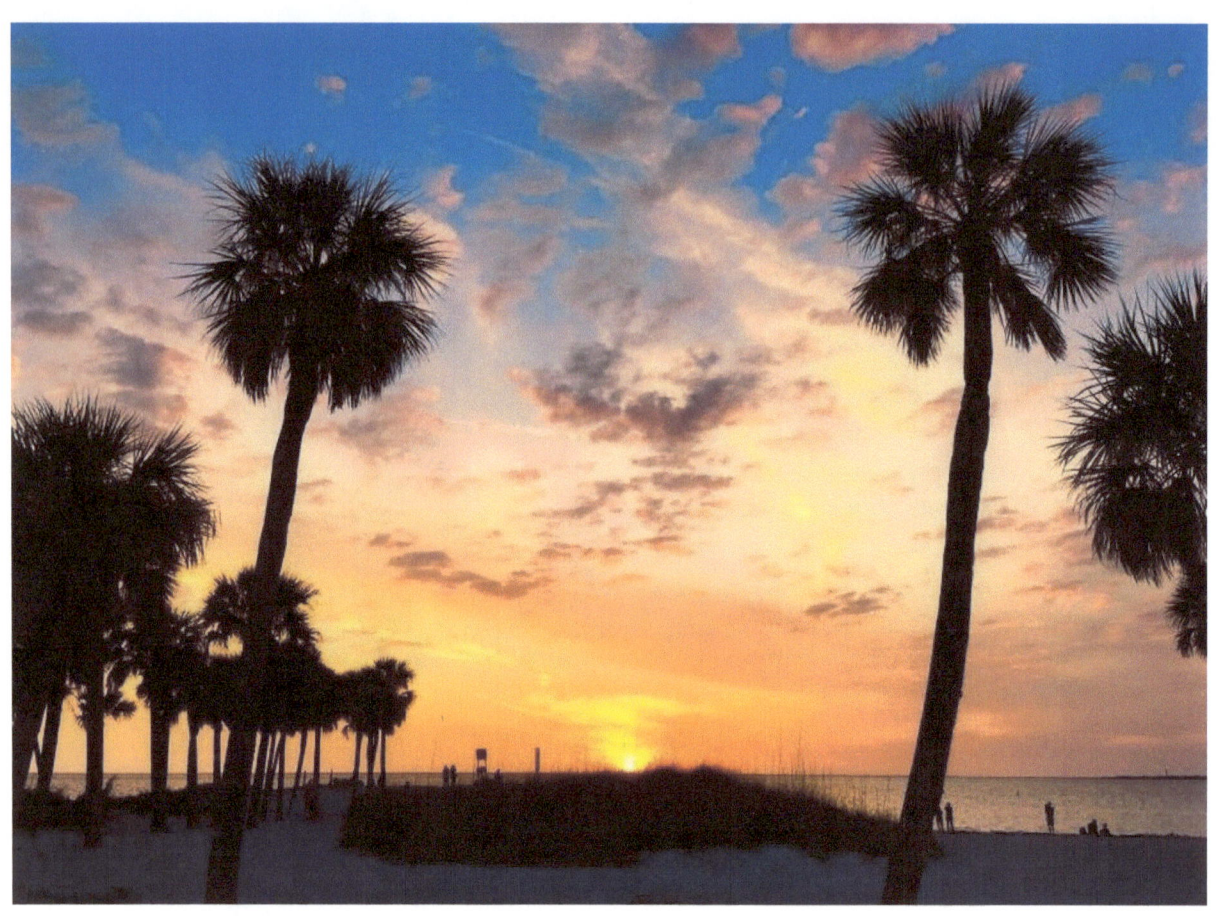

Port Richey Florida

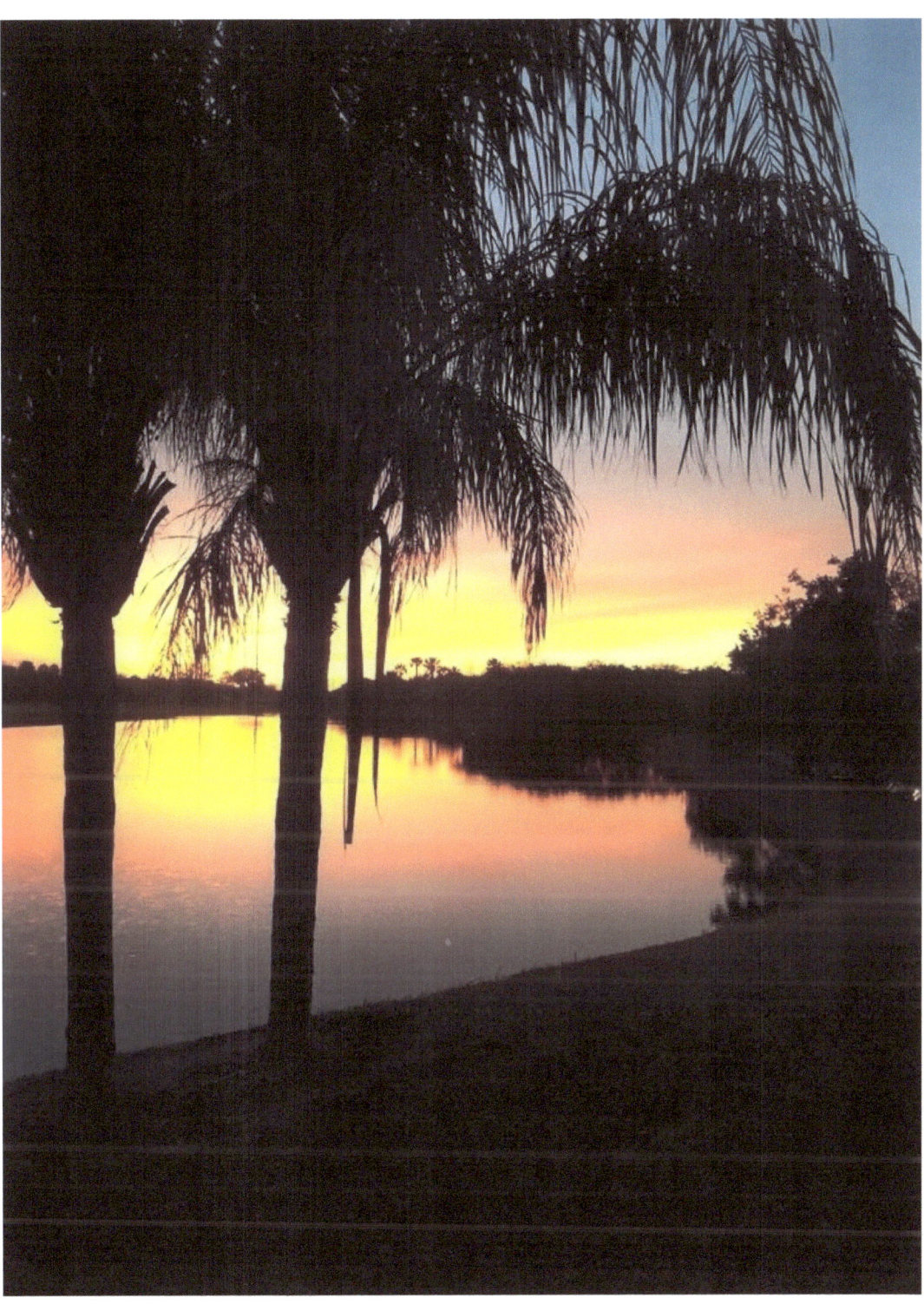

Tampa

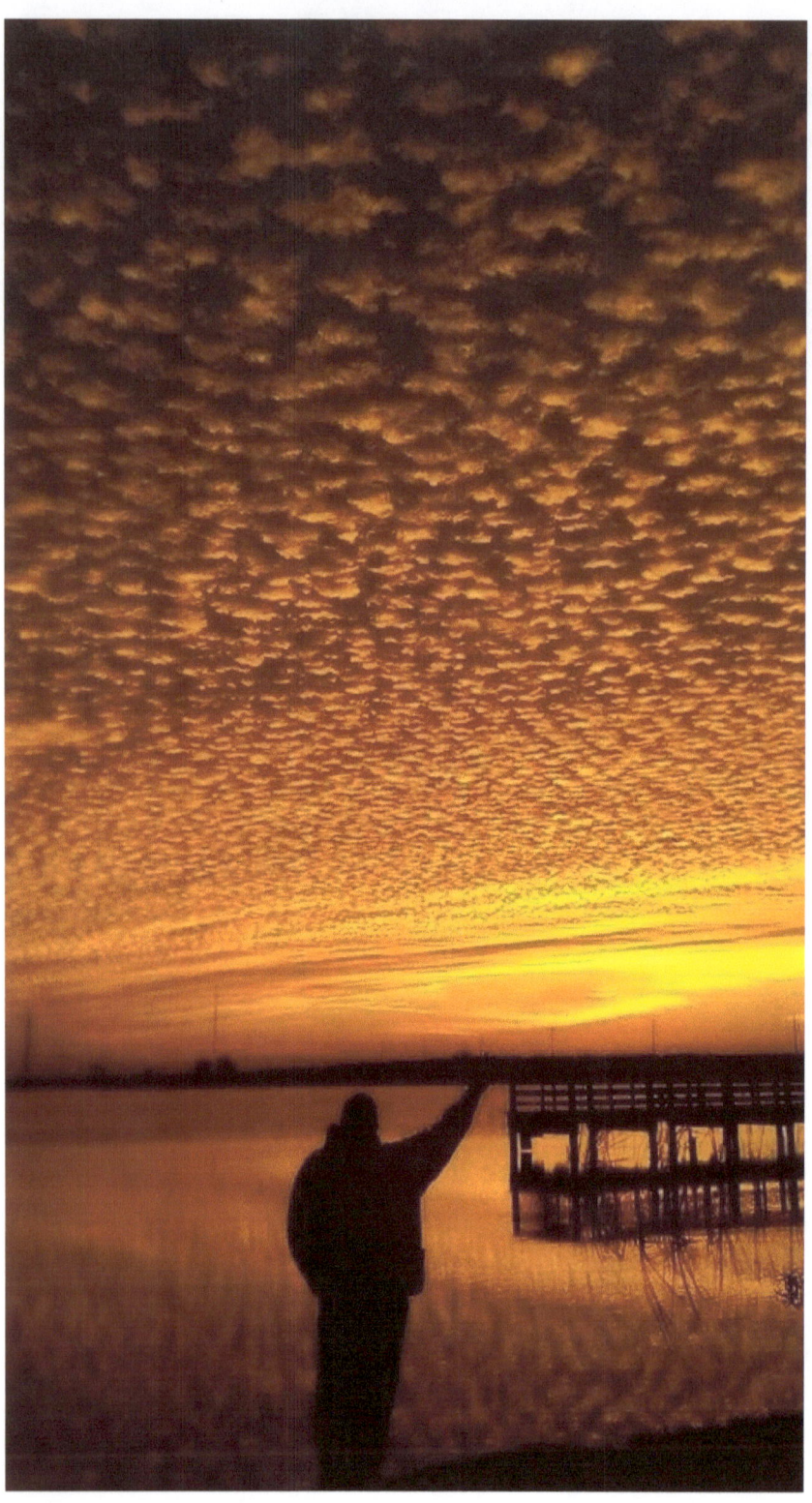

Melbourne Florida.

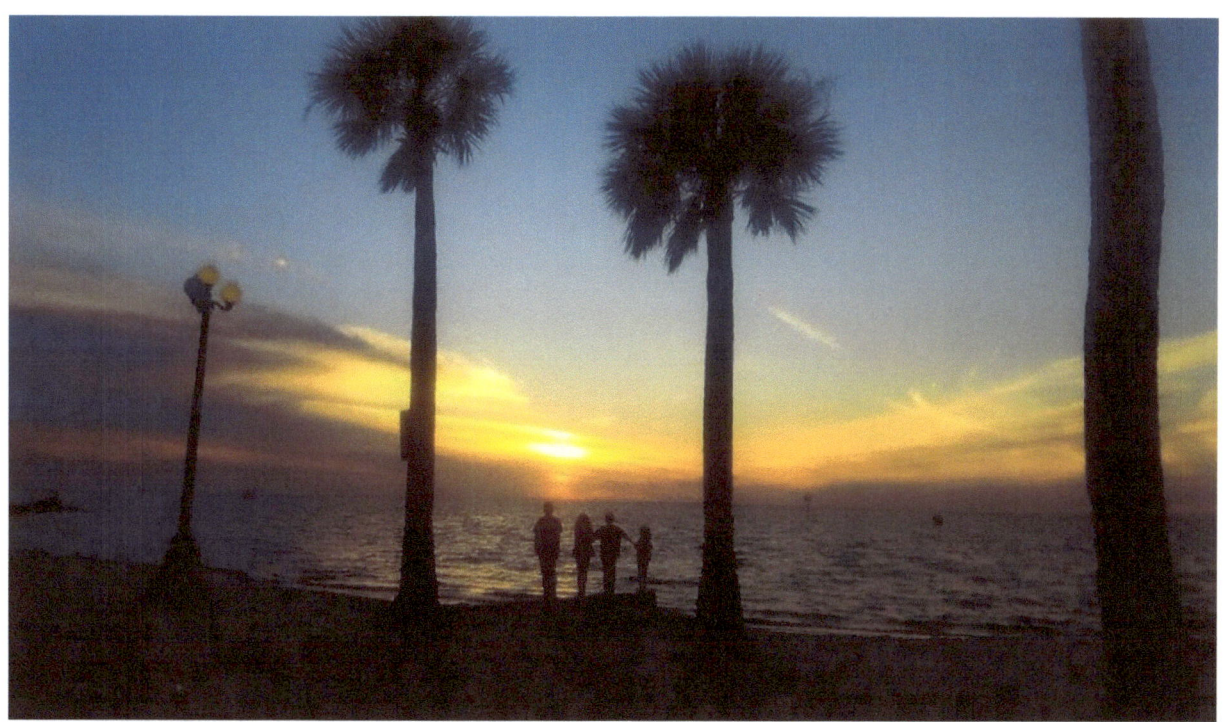

Port Richey Florida

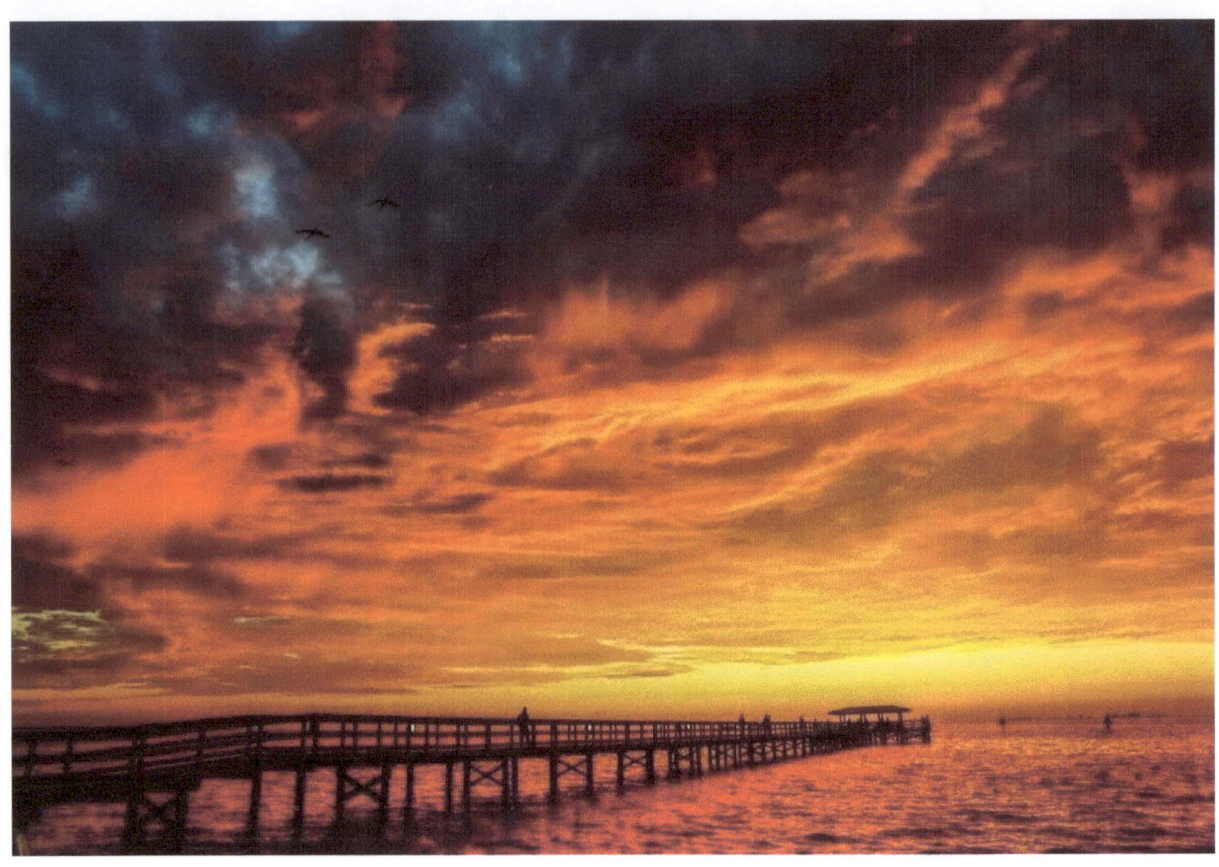

Tampa Florida

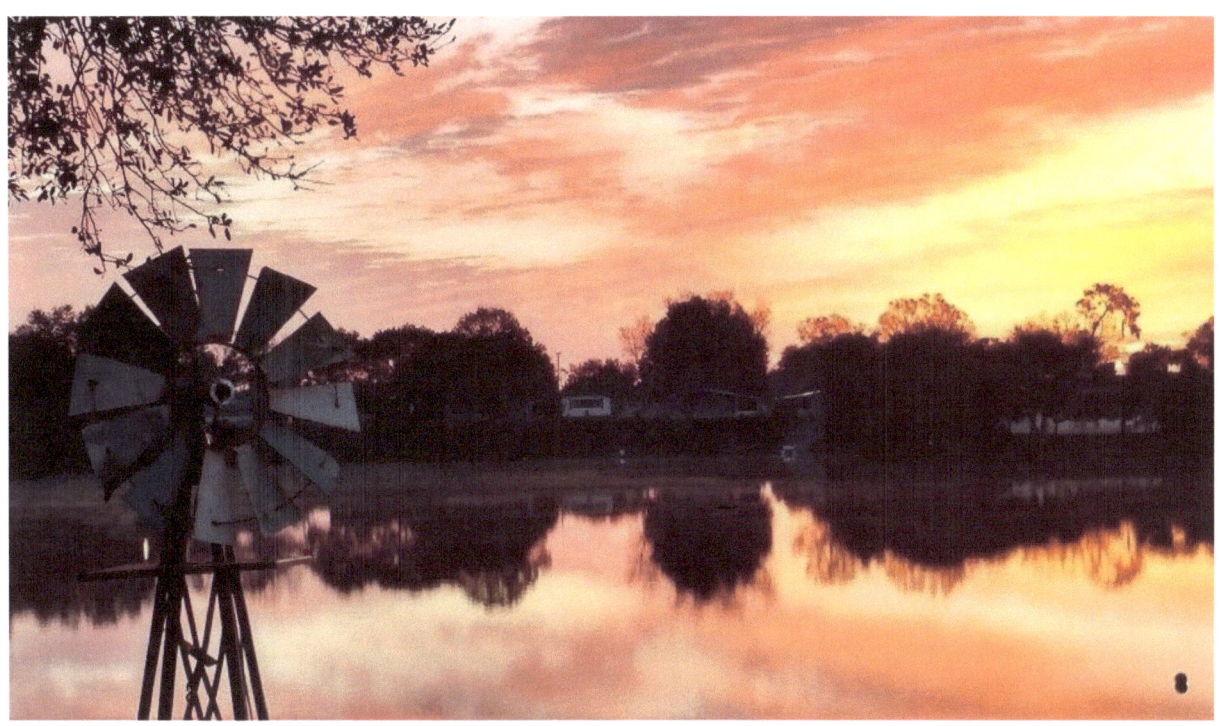

Lakeland Florida

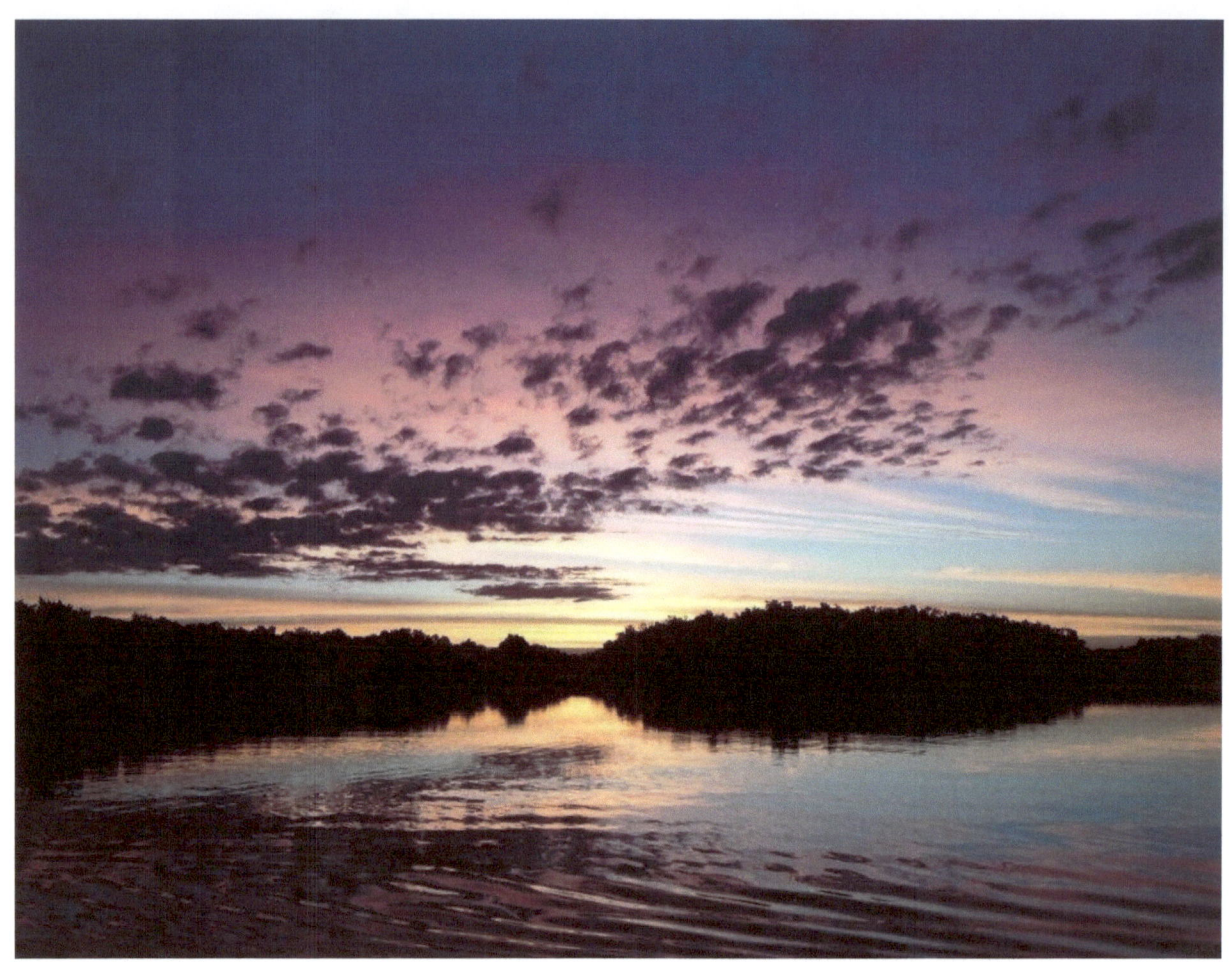

Lutz Fla

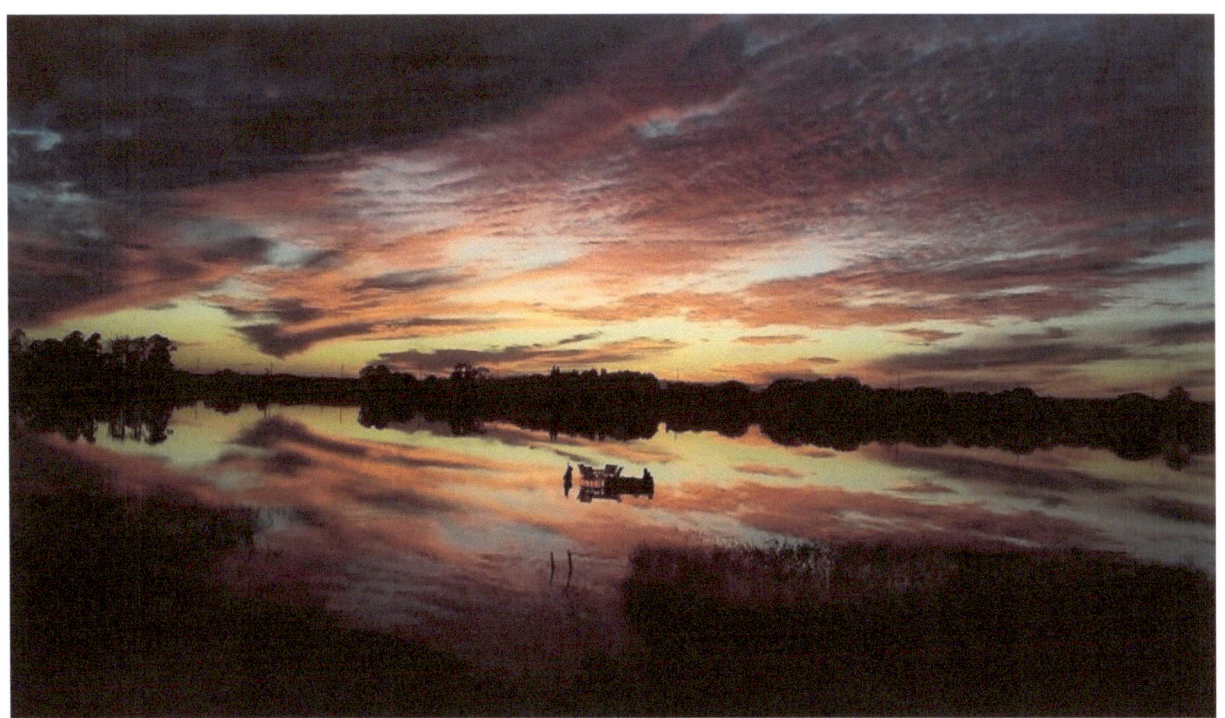

Orlando FL

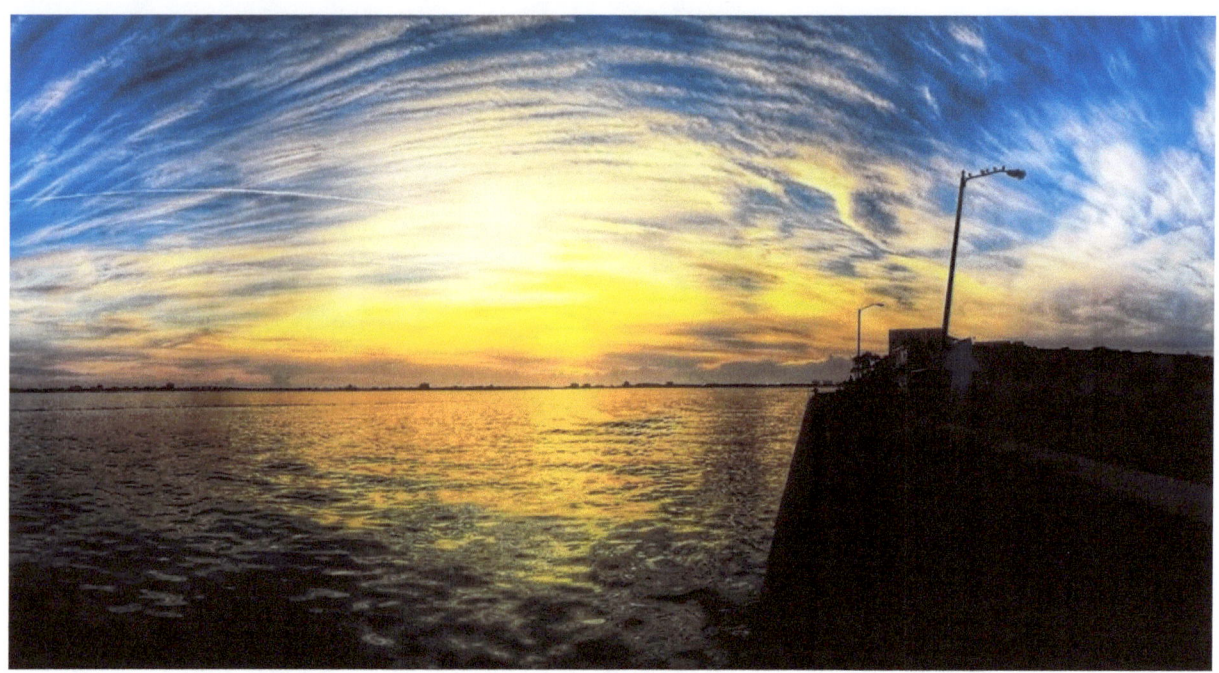

Daytona Beach FL

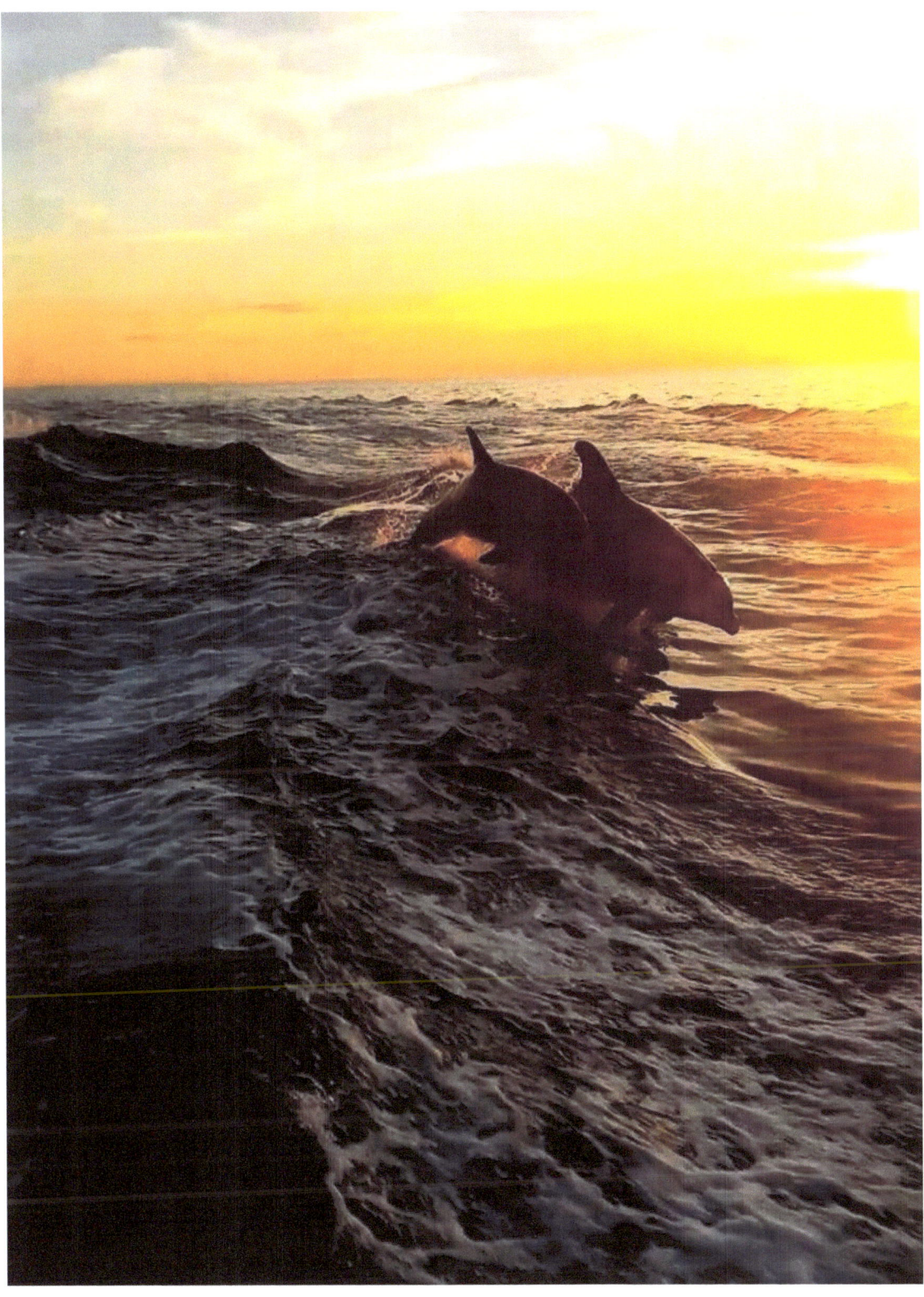

Clearwater Beach FL

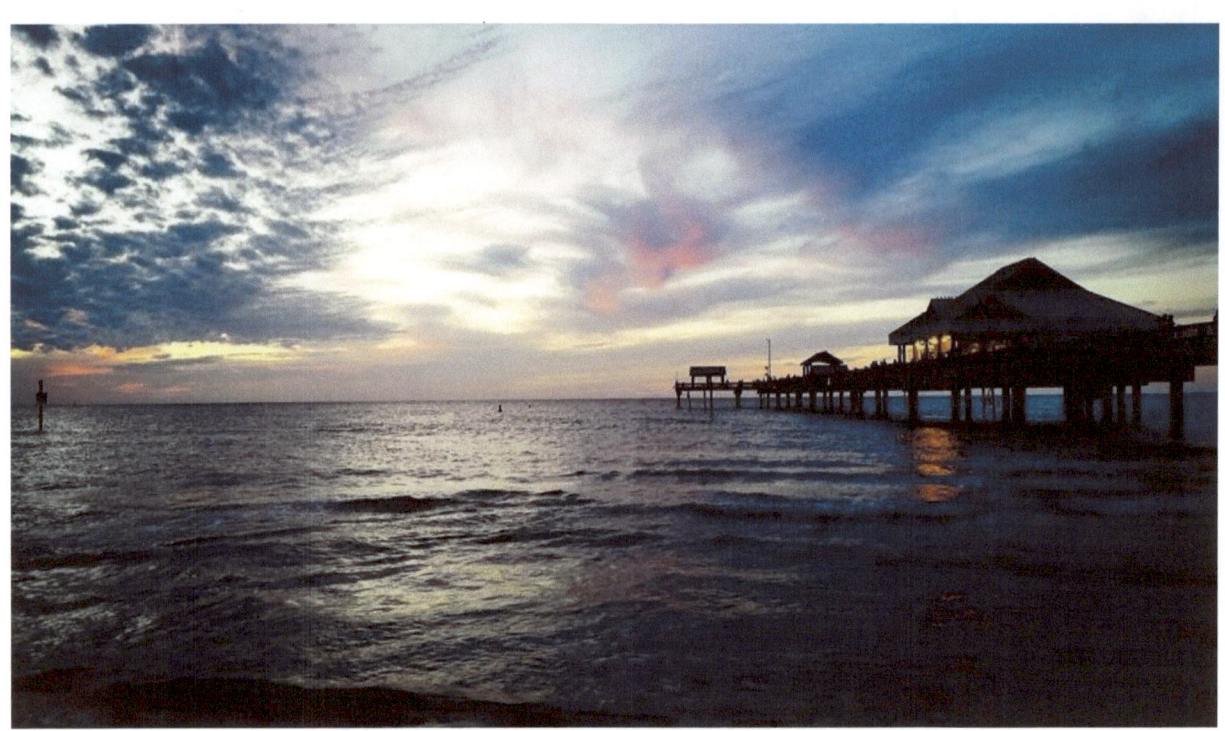

Port Richey FL

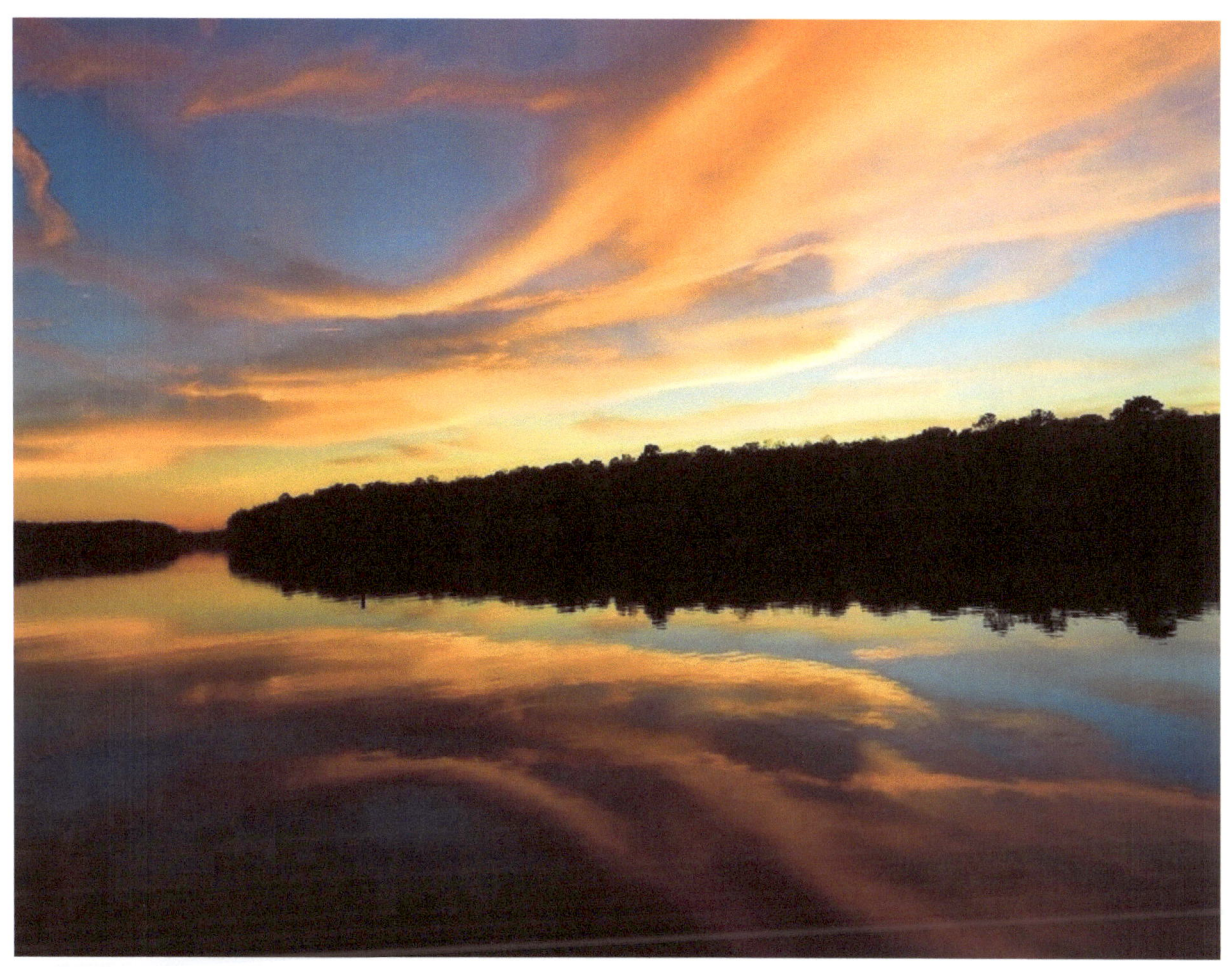

Lake Wales FL

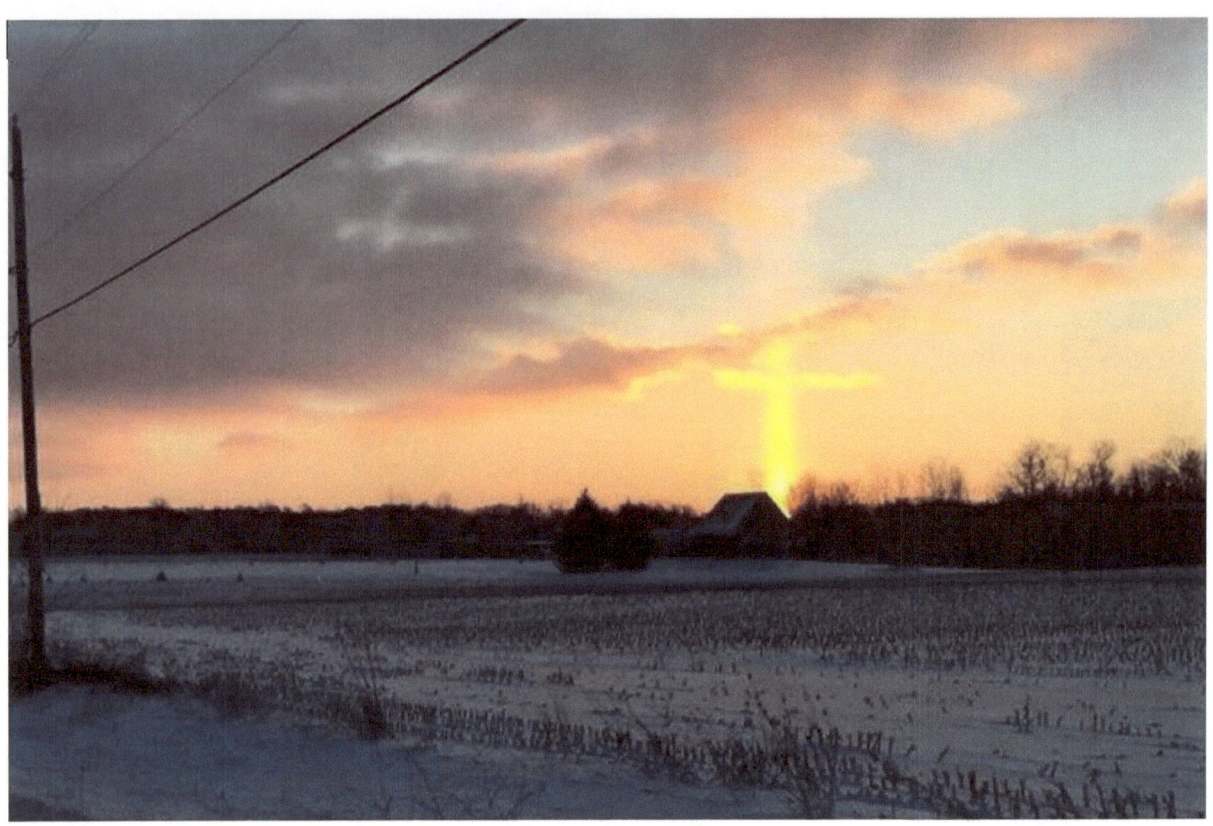

Port Richey FL

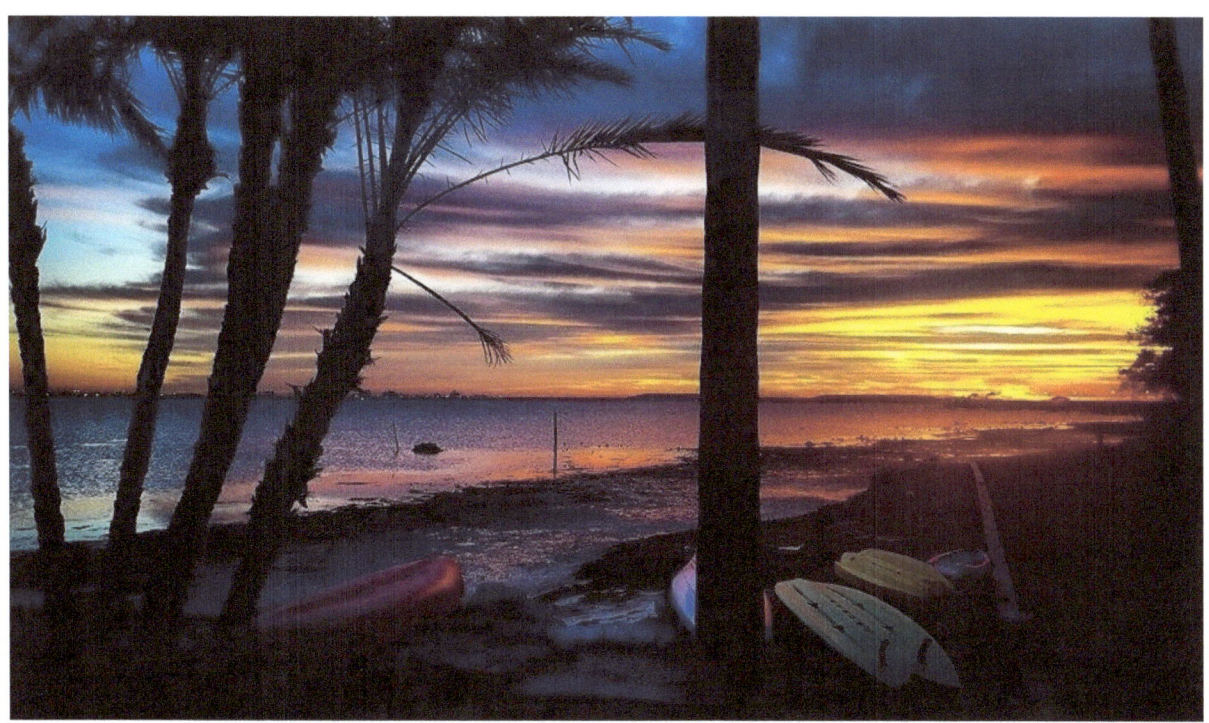

Clearwater FL

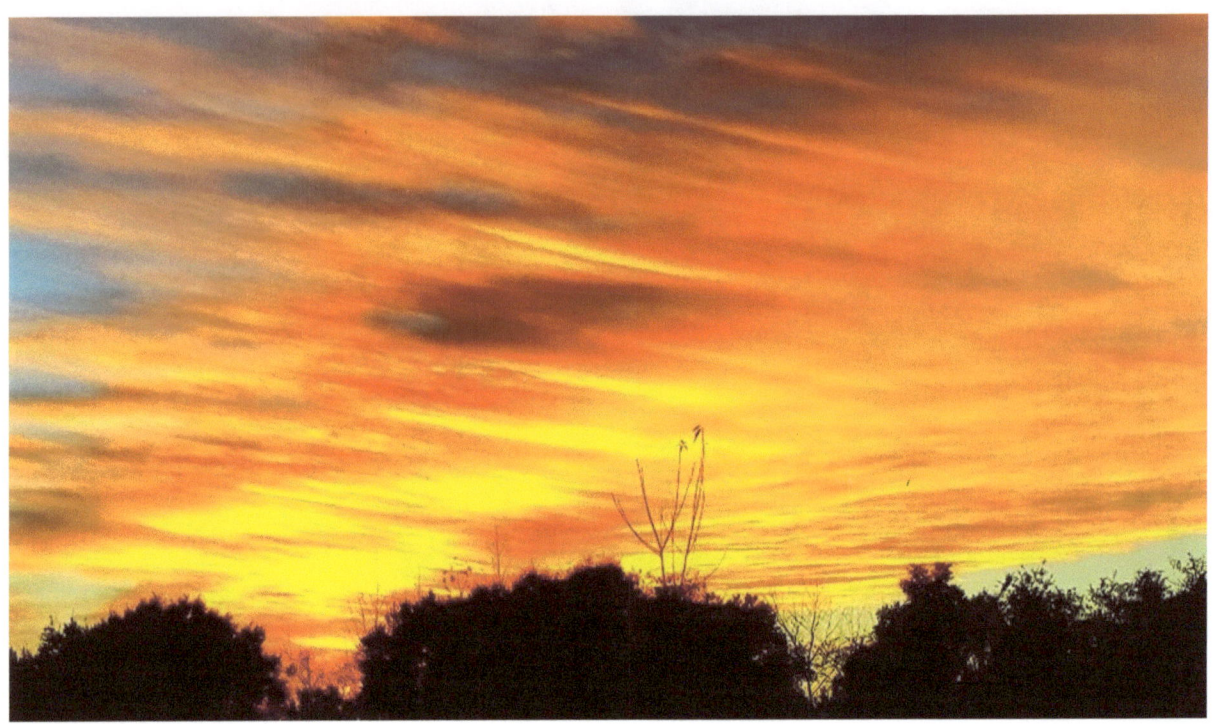

Leesburg FL

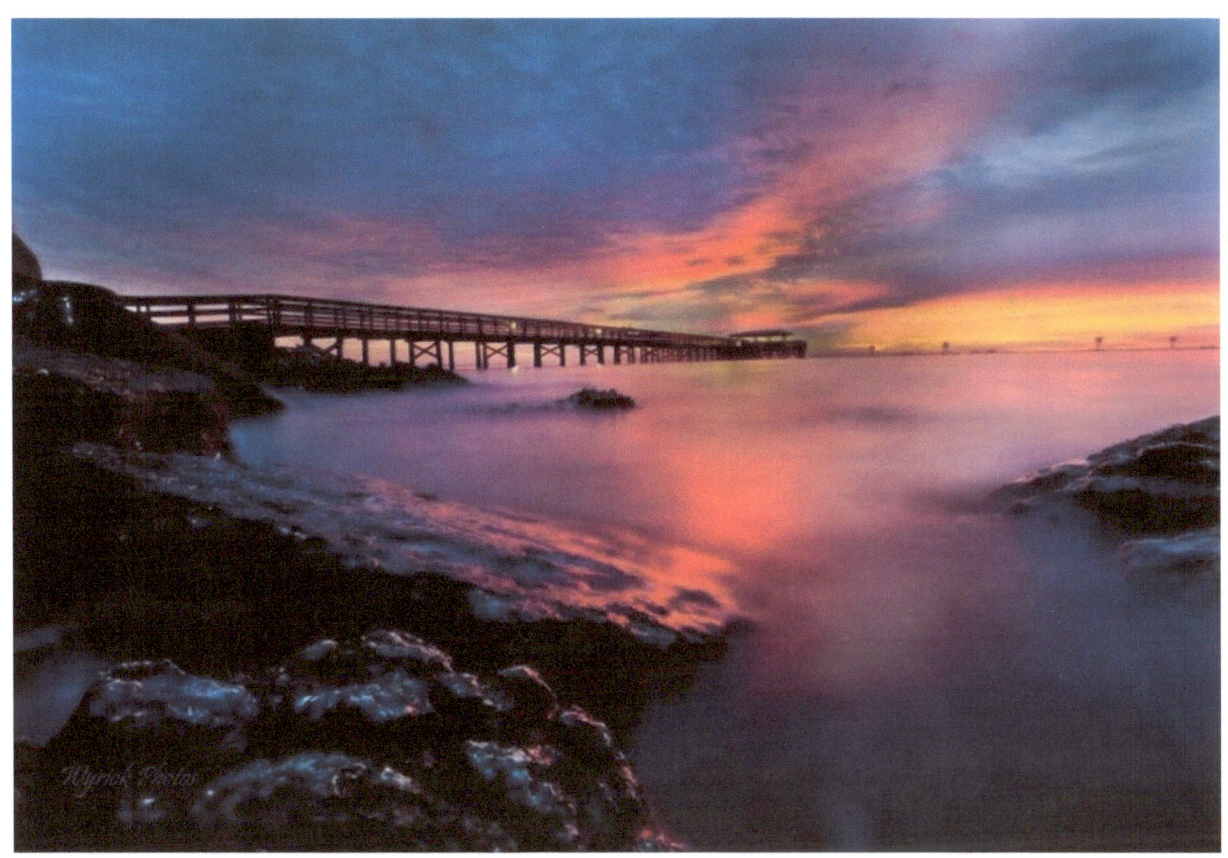

Melbourne FL

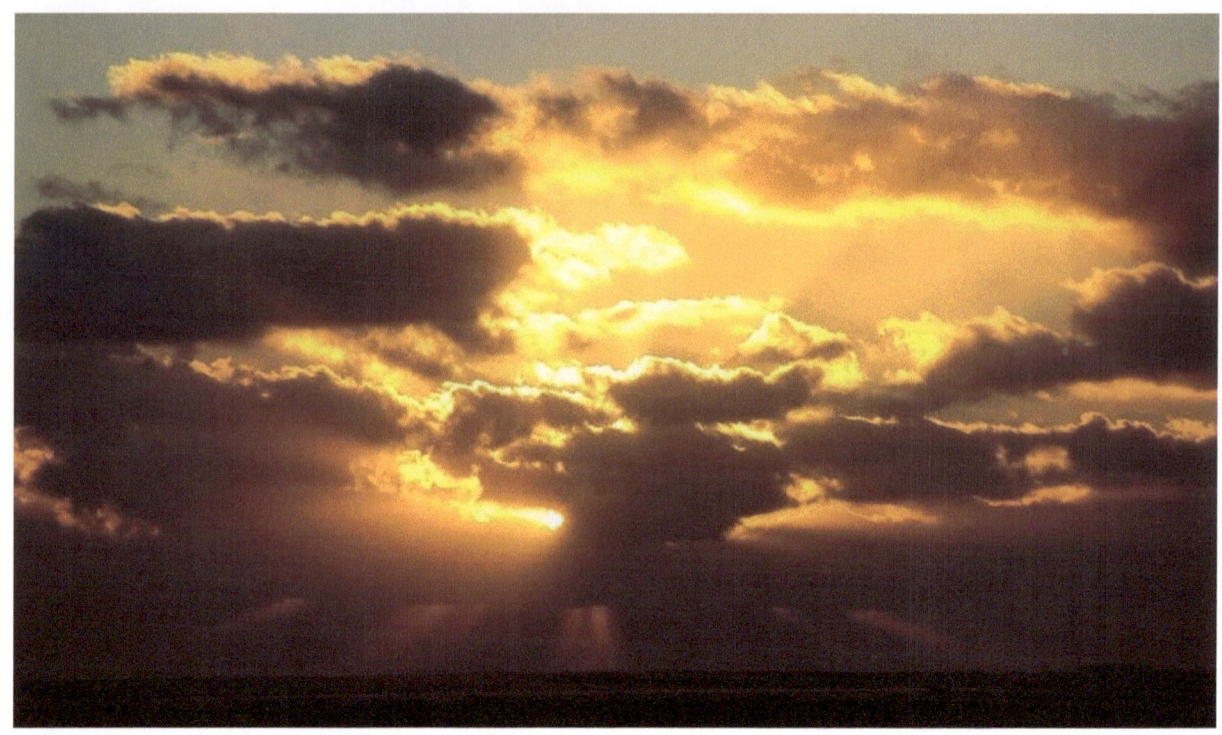

Port Richey FL

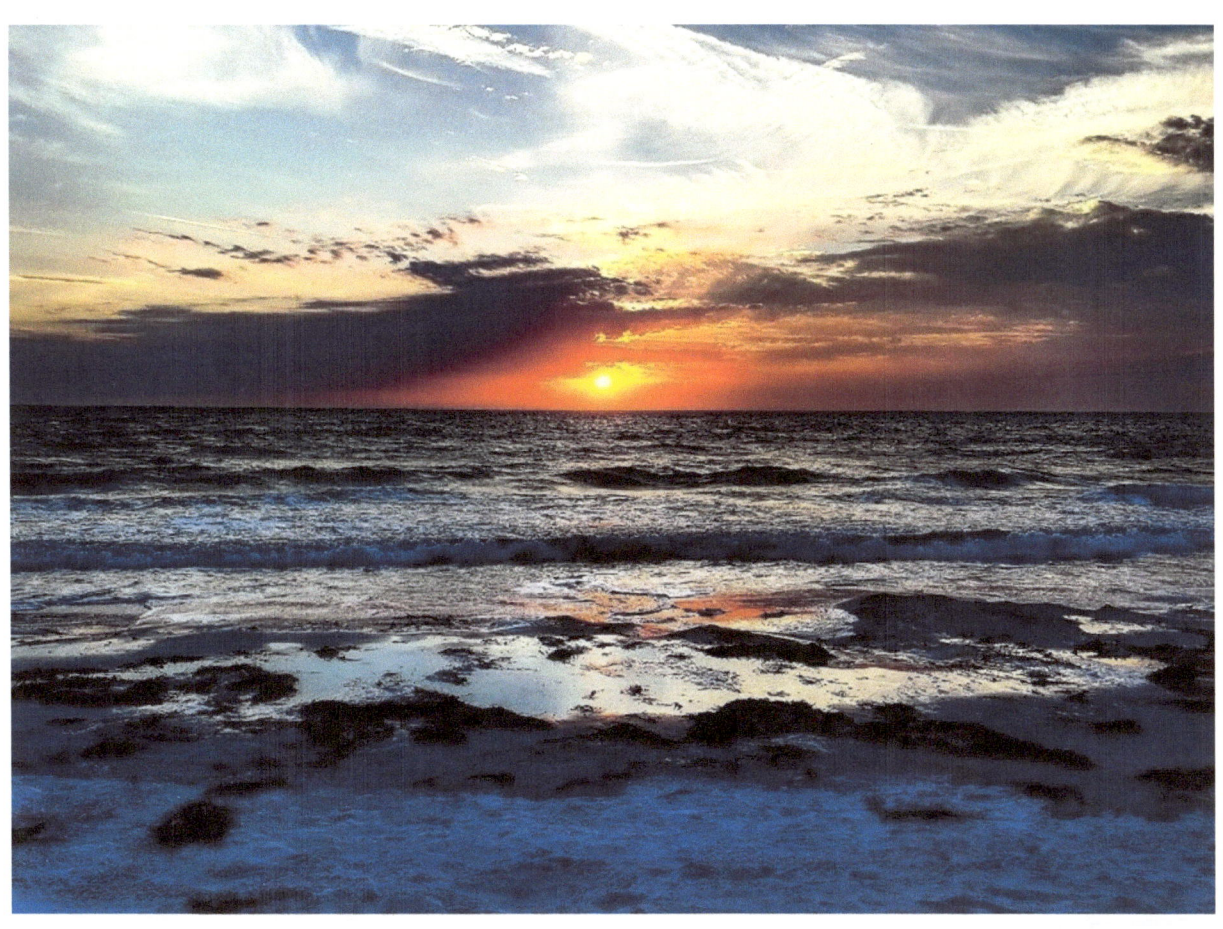

Tampa FL

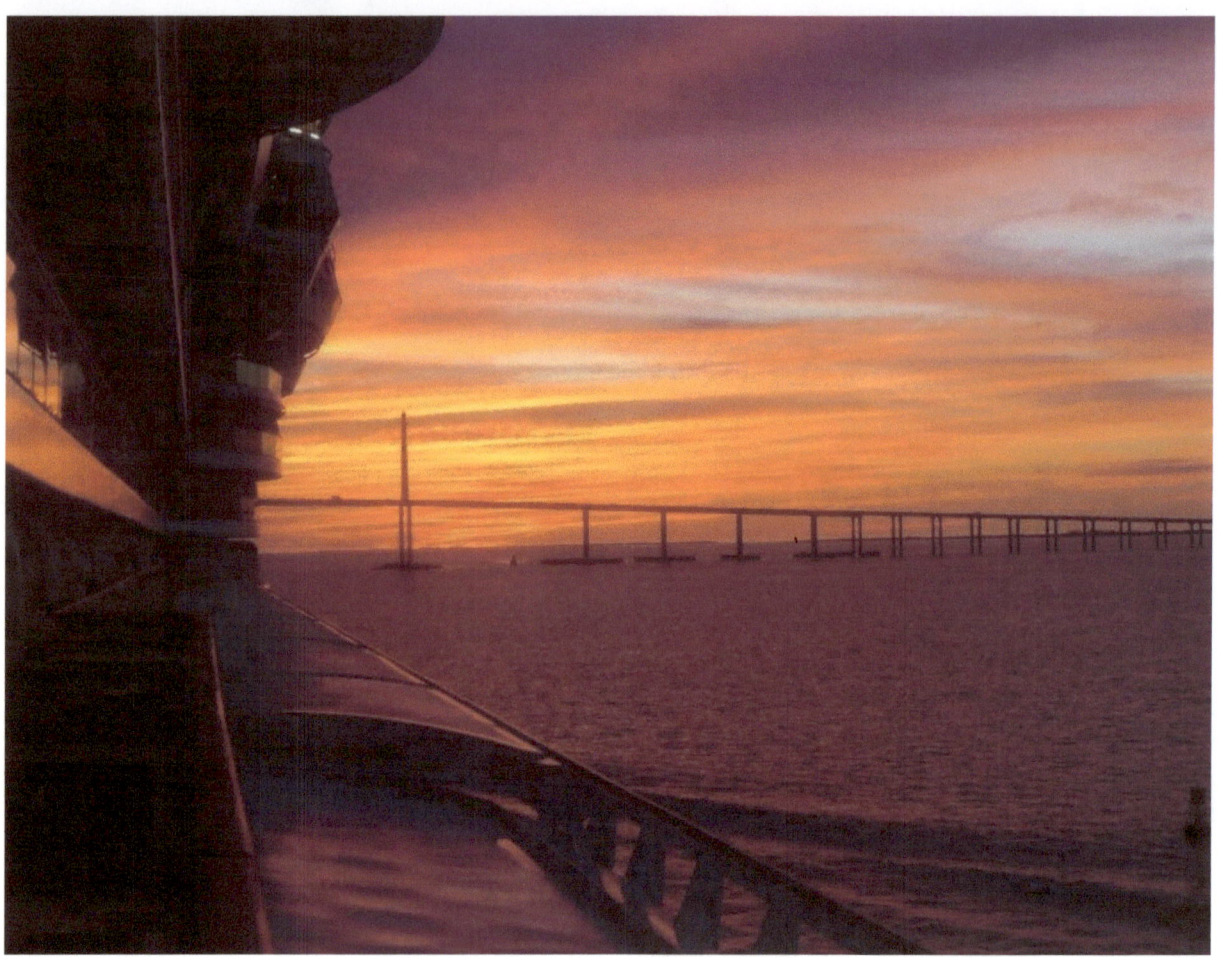

Tampa FL

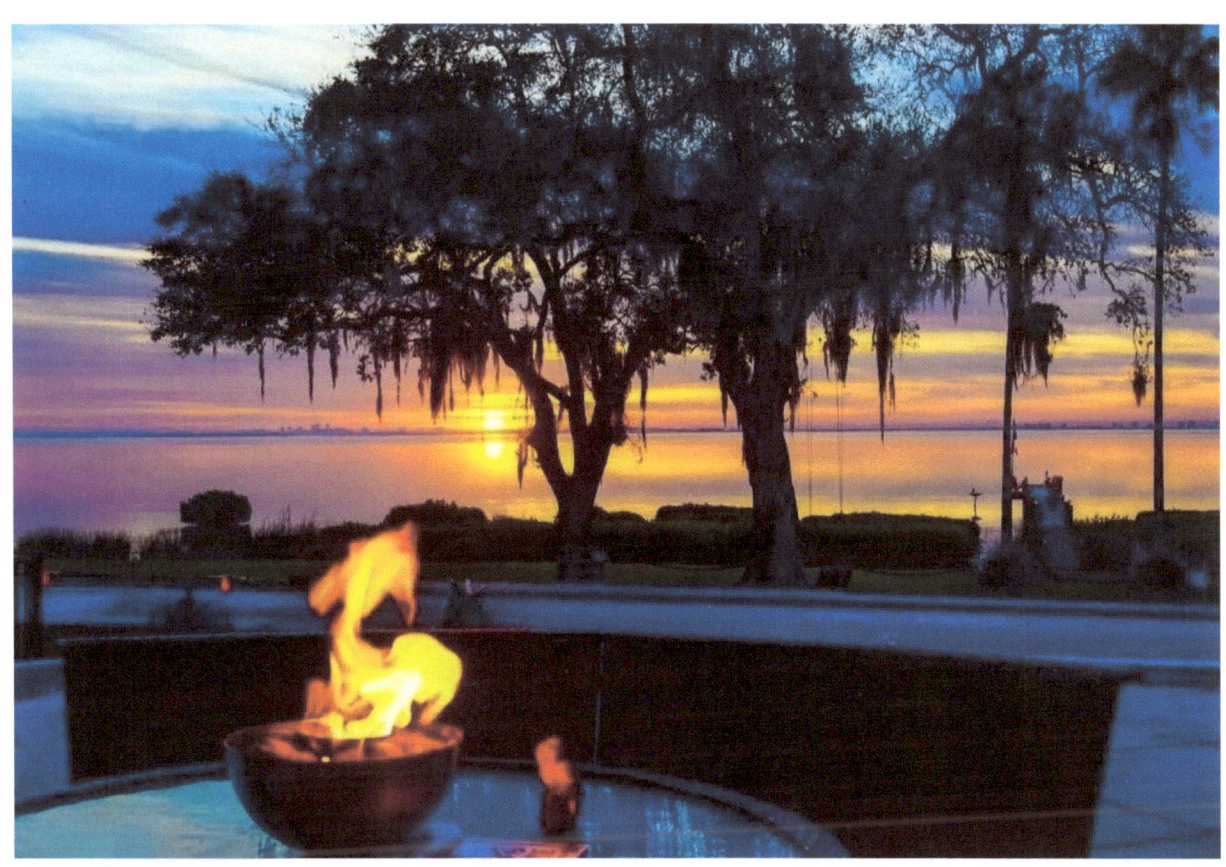

Tarpon Springs FL

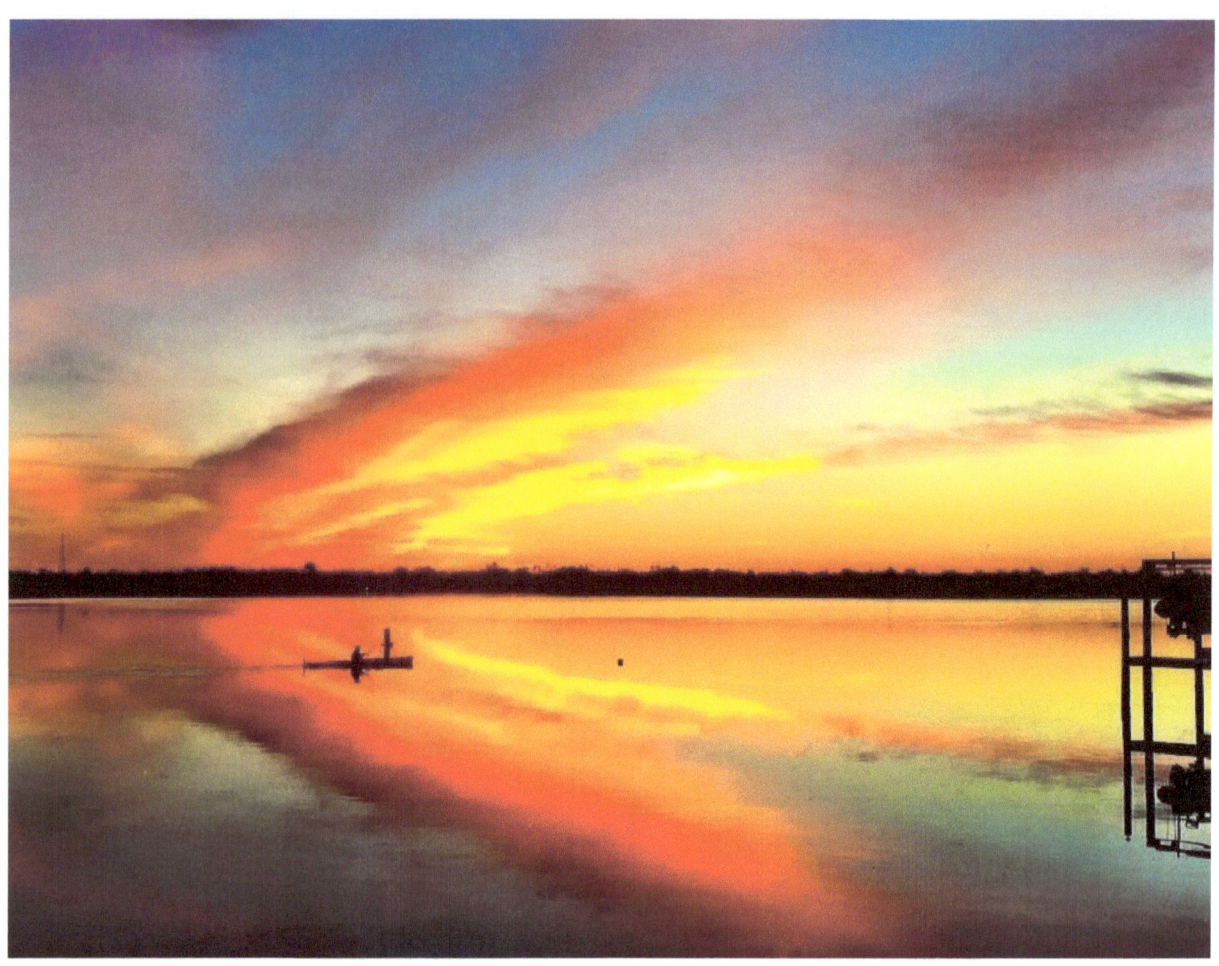

Tampa FL

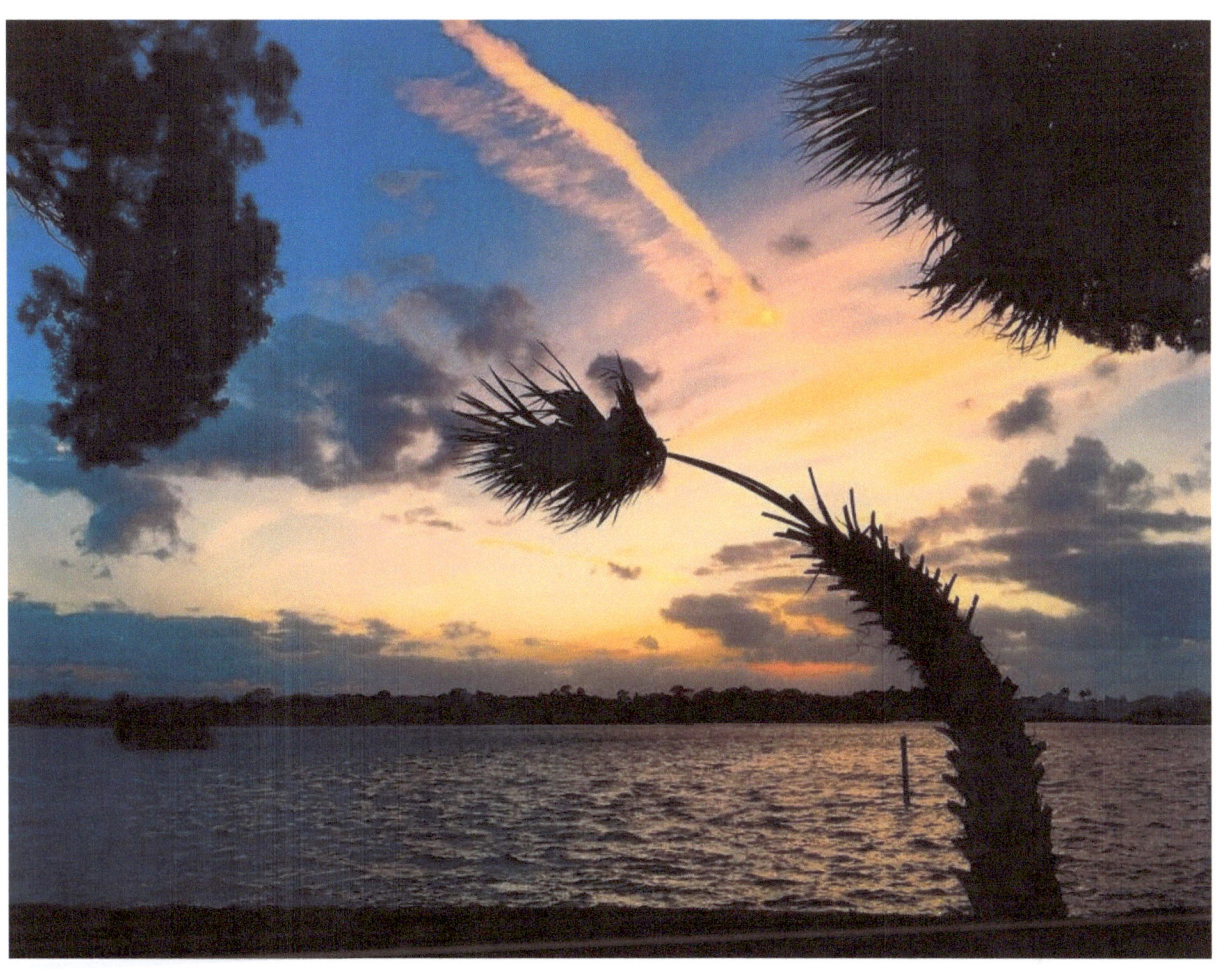

Port Richey FL

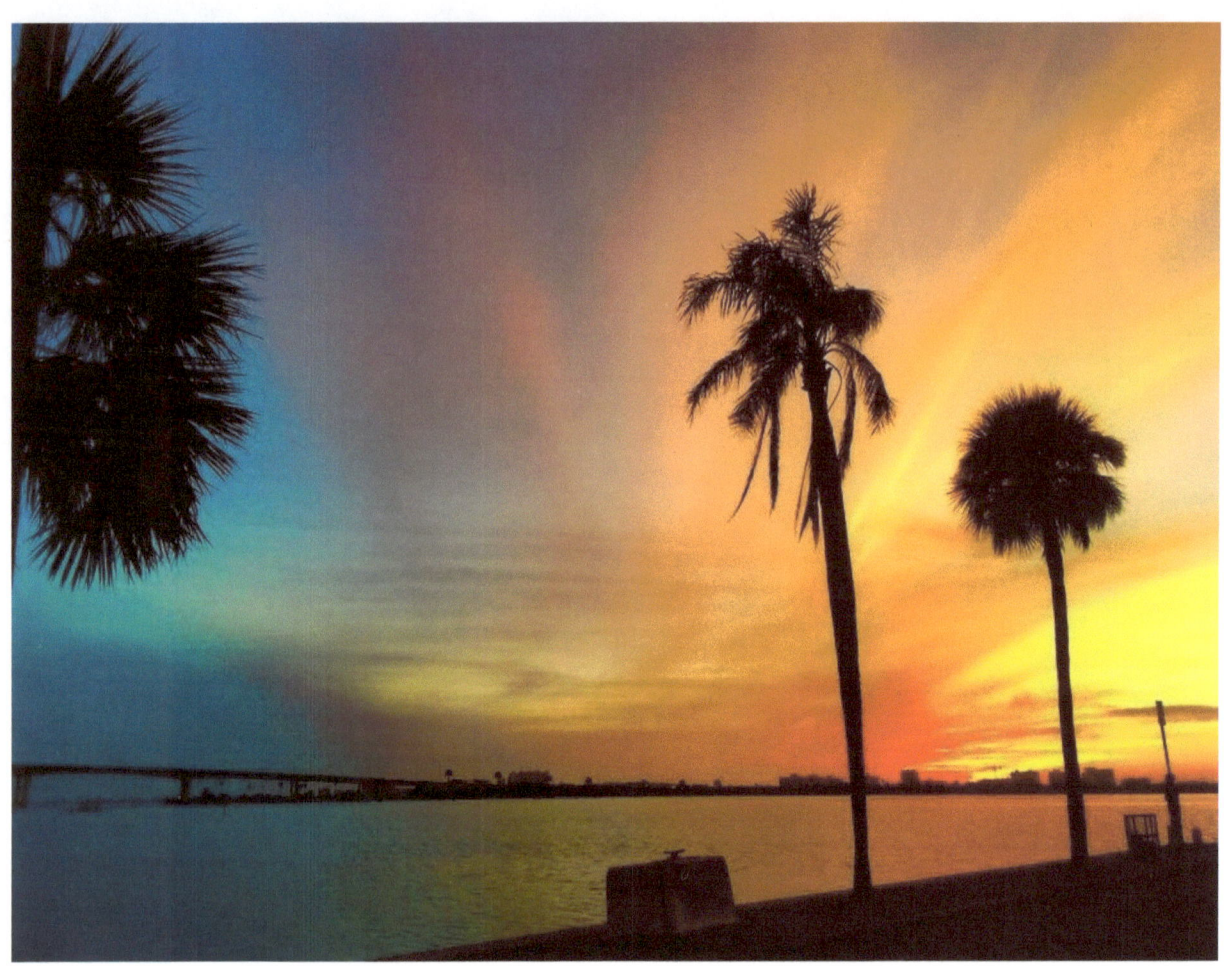

Port Richey FL

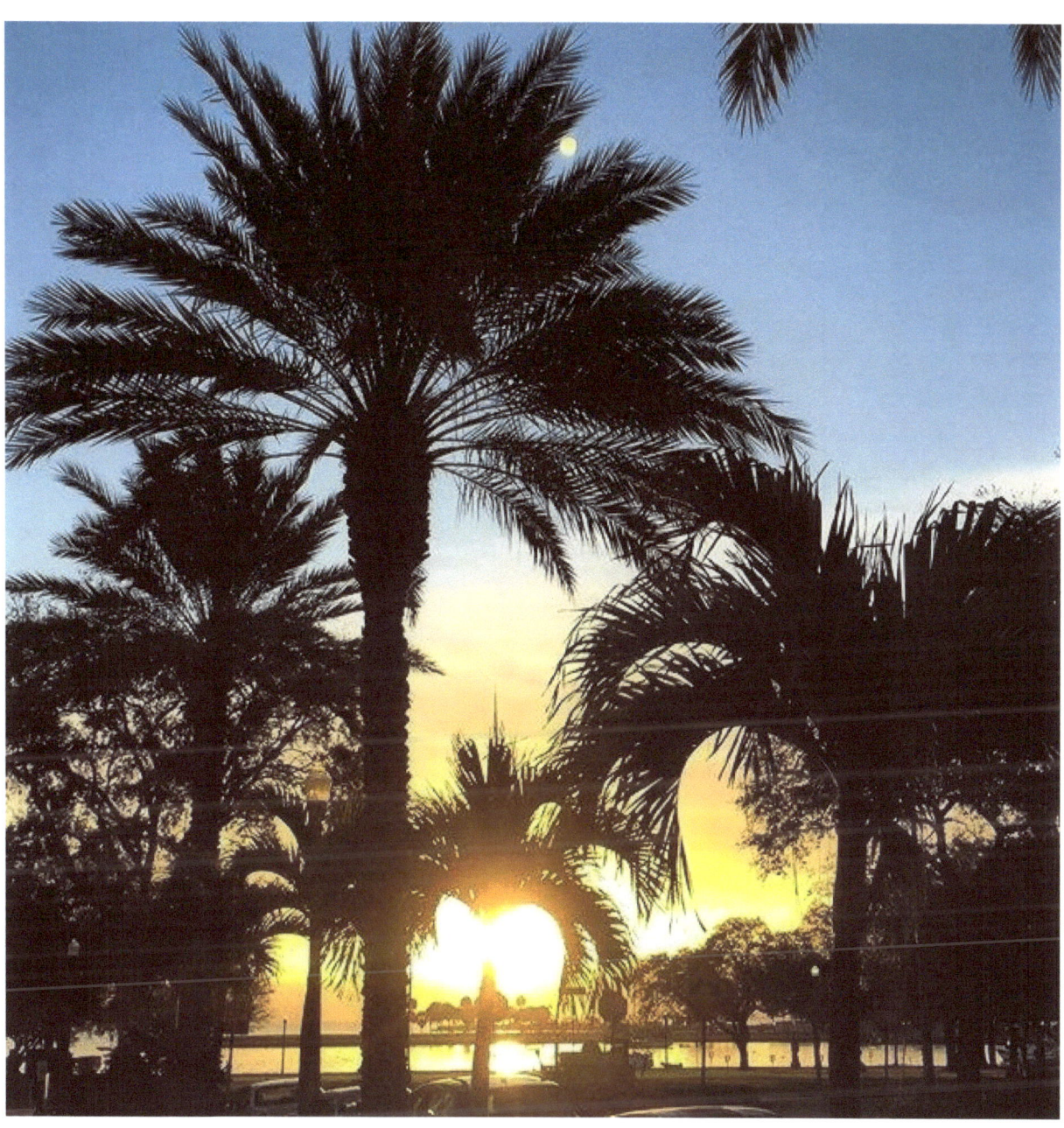

Melbourne FL

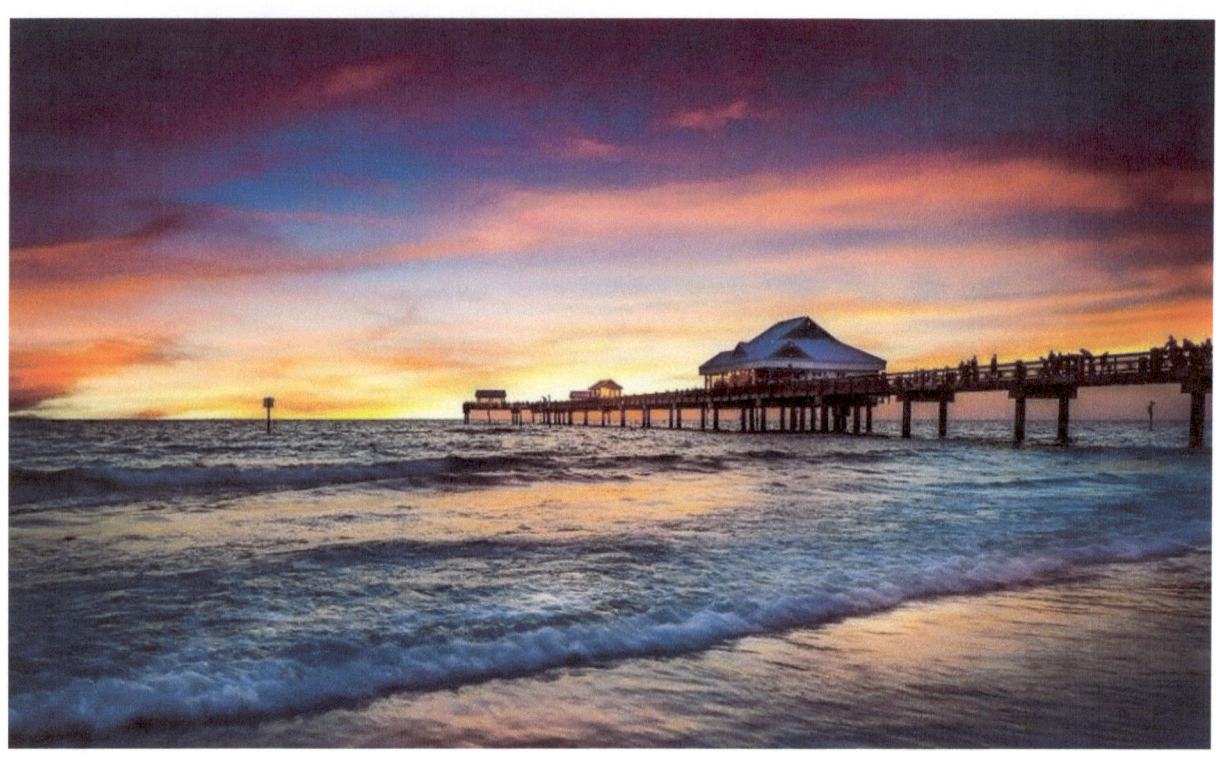

Clearwater FL

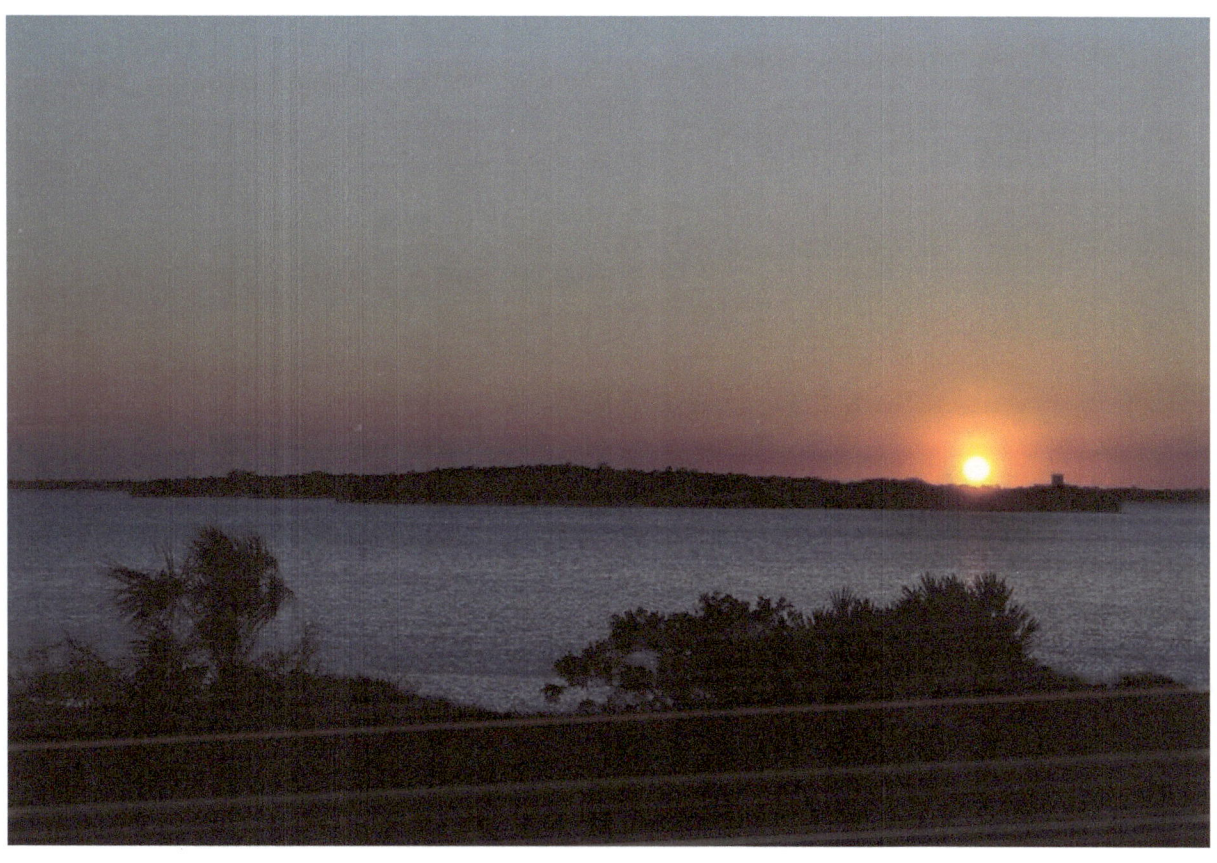

Honeymoon Island – FL

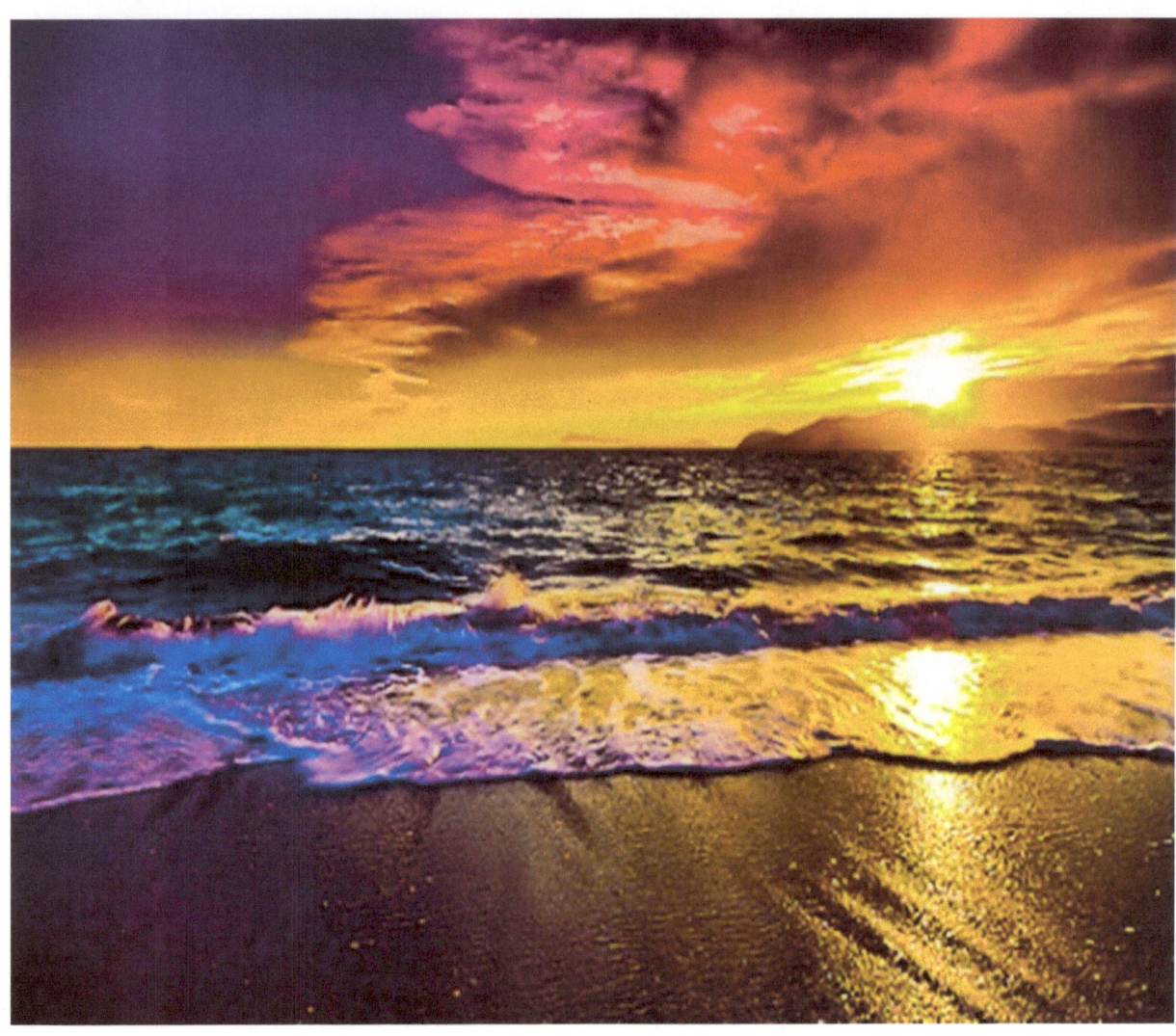

Port Richey Fl.